ACADEMIC PERFORMANCE OF COLLEGE STUDENTS

A SOCIO-PSYCHOLOGICAL PERSPECTIVE

ACADEMIC PERFORMANCE OF COLLEGE STUDENTS

A SOCIO-PSYCHOLOGICAL PERSPECTIVE

By

Dr. Anuradha Bansal

Assistant Professor
Deptt. of Sociology
Guru Nanak National College
Doraha (Ludhiana)

DISCOVERY PUBLISHING HOUSE PVT. LTD.
NEW DELHI-110 002

First Published-2010

ISBN 978-81-8356-651-3

Published by:

DISCOVERY PUBLISHING HOUSE PVT. LTD.
4831/24, Ansari Road, Prahlad Street
Darya Ganj, New Delhi-110002 (India)
Phone: +91-11-23279245, 43764432 • Fax: +91-11-23253475
E-mail: parul.wasan@gmail.com
info@discoverypublishinggroup.com
web: www.discoverypublishinggroup.com

Printed at:

Sachin Printers
Delhi

Dedicated

to

My Parents
who have Invested

Their Present
for My Future

ACKNOWLEDGEMENTS

It is my proud privilege to express my profound sense of gratitude and heartfelt thanks to my esteemed supervisor Prof. R.K. Choudhary, Former Head, Department of Sociology and Social Anthropology, Punjabi University, Patiala and Prof. (Retd.) G.S. Bhatnagar, for their enabling inspiration, valuable guidance, constructive criticism and constant encouragement which I received from them throughout the venture. I would like to place on record my sincere thanks to Dr. M.S. Randhawa who helped me in the initial stages of my research in designing and planning my work.

I will remain forever indebted to my beloved parents and other family members for their support, profound affection, positive attitude and whole-hearted co-operation without which this work could not have seen the light of the day. Those who deserve special mention are my dear brothers for helping me so much during the course of this study. They stood by me in the strongest winds.

I owe volumes of thanks to Mrs. Bhatnagar who gave me her unflinching support, love and confidence throughout this task.

I must put on record my sincere and deep sense of gratitude to my uncle, Dr. Davinder Kumar Singhal, for their valuable suggestions.

I can only remember with a feeling of gratitude, my respondents who willingly co-operated with me and earnestly responded to my queries.

ANURADHA BANSAL

CONTENTS

CHAPTER - I

INTRODUCTION AND REVIEW OF LITERATURE

STATEMENT OF THE RESEARCH PROBLEM

A historical analysis of the Indian society depicts that social inequalities existed in all historical periods, beginning from the Vedic period. The *varna* scheme devised during Rigvedic times was a mechanism to divide the society into groups of varying social status. The twice-born *varnas* were placed at higher level of hierarchy as compared to the shudra *varna*. This inequality in social status of various groups was linked to various facets of life, including the educational aspect. It was only the males of the higher three varnas (that is, Brahmins, Kshatriyas and Vaisyas) who were considered eligible to receive religious education in the *ashrams* of the *Rishis* or *Gurus*. The persons from Shudra *Varna* and females from all the four *varnas* were not considered eligible to receive education. Thus, the foundation of inequality in the educational sphere was laid in ancient India which has persisted even up to the contemporary period.

After India achieved independence, the Constitution of India guaranteed equal rights, in all spheres, to all the citizens of free India. However, a number of sociological researches have shown that this commitment could not be fully implemented in various spheres of social life, including the educational field. The social inequalities are mainly operative through the mechanism of the caste system. That is why most of the sociological researches on inequalities have concentrated only on the caste system. However, as a result of rapid and multi-faceted changes in the Indian society in recent years, caste is no longer the only basis of inequality. The educational and economic inequalities are assuming a more predominant role, although they are also in some ways related to the caste stratification. Therefore, it has been considered necessary in the present study to take into consideration both social and economic inequalities and their consequences on various aspects of social life. The proposed research seeks to investigate the impact of socio-economic inequalities on the achievement motivation and academic performance of college students, both from rural and urban areas. Before the objectives of the study are stated, it will be pertinent to briefly describe the concepts of achievement motivation and academic performance.

The concept of achievement motivation was put forth by Murry (1938). However, the studies of McClelland added a practical dimension to this concept which can be used in various fields of research, including education. Generally speaking, achievement motivation (also referred as need for achievement) is the desire of a person to excel others in performance. Thus, it can be considered as the wish of an individual to perform well. Motivation to achieve is aroused when an individual knows that he is responsible for the outcome of some venture, when he anticipates explicit knowledge or results that will define his success or failure and when there is some degree of risk, that is, some uncertainty about he outcome of his effort. The goal of achievement oriented activity is to succeed, to perform well in relation to a standard of excellence in comparison with others who are competitors. (McOllelland 1961, Atkinson 1964).

The researches in Psychology have shown that individuals differ in the degree of their achievement motivation. These studies emphasize the personality factors to account for the variations in the achievement motivation of individuals. Some studies in the field of Social Psychology have revealed the importance of family and socio-economic status as being contributory factors in achievement motivation. (Mehta, 1969; Chaudhary, 1971 and Gokulnathan and Mehta, 1972).

The academic performance of a student is generally measured through the percentage of marks obtained by him in examinations. This gives an overall idea about the scholastic achievements which are considered as indicators of intelligence. The academic achievement of a student is the major aspect of present education. The performance in this field might be influenced by a variety of social and psychological factors. In the proposed study an effort will be made to investigate the role of socio-economic factors (like caste, economic status, place of residence, type of family, educational and economic levels of the family) in affecting the achievement motivation and academic performance of college students.

CONCEPTUAL AND THEORETICAL FRAMEWORK

Achievement Motivation

Long ago, Bentham (1879) had described a motive as "a pleasure, pain, or other event, that prompts to action." Many psychologists likewise, postulated an antecedent state of emotion which initiated and directed behaviour. Freud (1920) too regarded 'wish' as an emotionally charged idea which, like an irritant, initiated behaviour. However, such mentalistic interpretations soon gave way to the notion of 'drive' which attributed the initiation of goal-directed behaviour to arousal conditions. In Newcomb's (1950) words, "an organism (O) is motivated when-and only when it is characterised both by a state of drive and by a direction of behaviour towards some goal, which is selected in preference to all other possible goals. Motive, then, is a concept which joins together "drive and goal".

Drever (1952) described a motive "as an affective-conative factor which operates in determining the direction of an individual's behaviour towards on end or goal, consciously apprehended, or unconscious". Young (1961) defined it as, "process of arousing action, sustaining the activity progress, and regulating the pattern of activity." Motives determine why people behave as they do, they are the genotypes of behaviour. Motives are the causes of behaviour. A motive "is a strong affective state associated and characterised by an anticipatory goal reaction and based upon past association of certain cues with pleasure or pain." (McClelland, 1951) Later, McClelland and his associates (McClelland *et al.*, 1953) defined a motive as the "reintegration by a cue of a change in an affective situation", which signifies that "an affective state can be reinstated in consciousness if it has been stimulated by an environmental cue."

A motive or a need is "a disposition to strive for a particular kind of goal, state or aim, for example, achievement or power". (Atkinson, 1958) The aim of particular motive is the particular kind of 'effect' to be brought about through some kind of action or the 'kind' of satisfaction sought, for example, pride in accomplishment, a positive affective relationship with another person, a sense of being in control of the means of influencing the behaviour of the other persons. He further clarifies that whereas "motive" refers to more general and relatively stable disposition; 'motivation' signifies a 'temporarily aroused state', produced when the cues of a situation elicit an expectancy of goal attainment which engages the motive.

The 'need' is a construct, indistinguishable from 'motive' which stands for a force in the brain-region, a force which organises perception, apperception, contains an action in such a way as to transform in a certain direction the existing, unsatisfying situation (Murry, 1938).

In order to deal with the enormity of human needs, psycholgists have classified them into two general categories, that is, biological needs and social needs. The former originate out of basic biological demands for food, water, oxygen, etc. and the later refer to the needs for achievement, social status, self-esteem etc. The needs fluctuate in dominating the individual's behaviour. Whereas, the biological needs are considered to be essential for survival, the social needs are learned by particular interaction with people (each individual serving as a stimulus source for the other) and the environment. As a matter of fact, once these needs are learned, they assume the same importance for the maintenance of the normal health of an individual as do the biological needs.

Traditionally, motivation has been defined as the control of behaviour, that is, the process by which behaviour is activated and directed toward some definable goal (Young, 1961). The specific nature of the control varies widely according to the behaviour. Thus, the control mechanism involves in simple reflexes, and in eating and drinking, in attachment and aggression, in curiosity and exploration which are quite different from one another.

Atkinson (1968) defines n-Ach as a capacity to experience pride in accomplishment. Further, in his words, "achievement motivation is an important determinant of aspiration effort, and persistence when an individual expects that his performance will be evaluated in relation to some standard of excellence." The antecedents of individual differences in the n-Ach have been of considerable interest to those working with this motive. Marked differences can be presumed to be present among cultures or even among families within a culture in terms of their stress on achievement or success.

Motivation involves two basic functions - one, an arousal or energizing function which mobilizes the bodily resources for vigorous and intense response, and the other, a directive function which guides behaviours to specific ends. This explains why individuals behave in a particular manner at a particular time or choose particular goals and not others. As these two functions are not mutually exclusive, behaviour at any one time is the result of the integration of both these aspects of motivation.

Heckhausen (1967) defined n-Ach as "the striving to increase or keep as high as possible one's own capability in all activities in which a standard of excellence is thought to apply and where the execution of such activities can, therefore, either succeed or fail".

According to Hebb (1972) motivation is a "tendency of the whole organism to produce organized activity, normally varying from the low level of deep sleep to a high level in the walking, alert, excited organism and varying also in the kind of behaviour that results or the kind of stimulation to which the organism is responsive."

In other words, all the systems in the hierarchy are relatedly structured to perform certain critical functions; and simultaneously, these system are progressively more open to the influence of individual experience. Motivation, emotion, curiosity and exploring the environment, help to understand the behaviour of an individual as these are important functions of the individual's experience.

Two broad approaches to the study of achievement motivation can be identified in the literature. One approach, associated with the work of McClelland and his co workers (1961), has sought the origins of n-Ach (the commonly accepted abbreviation for 'need for achievement) in studies of child rearing practices, and the consequences of n-Ach in cross-cultural comparisons which relate n-Ach to indices of economic development. Measures of n-Ach developed by McClelland *et.al.*, (1953) are typically projective type tests such as the Thematic Apperception Test (T.A.T.) by means of which the tests reveals his unconscious needs for achievement. Several disadvantages have been noted in the use of projective type measures. The other approach to the study of achievement motivation, springing from the work of Atkinson (1965) and his associates, has focused upon psychological theories of motivation as a means of deepening our understanding of need for achievement. Atkinson's Conceptualization of a n-Ach differentiates between the motive to succeed and the motive to avoid failure, seeking to explain achievement in light of this differentiation and the perceived probability of success in a specified task.

McClelland *et al.*, (1953) carried out both qualitative and quantitative studies of the TAT (Thematic Appreciation Test) stories written by their subjects. In general, the results were positive in the sense that the higher the level of the achievement motive, the greater were the number of achievement responses in the TAT. There were, of course, instances of failure and a mixed type of imagery revealed in the stories.

McClelland (1961) later extended his theory of achievement motivation into the area of society as a whole. The 'achieving society', he suggests, is not especially favoured by population growth, economic conditions, or natural resources, but is high in achievement motivation. The entrepreneurial spirit, the presence of executive with high level of drive, and a social orientation that emphasizes achievement in the training of children are the factors necessary for high levels of achievement in a society.

According to McClelland (1951), "motive involves two points on an affective continuum: a present state (either positive, negative, or neutral) which redintegrates, through past learning, a second state involving an increase or decrease in pleasure or pain in the present state". Taken in this perspective, motives are aroused in situations in which there are discrepancies between the present affective state and an expected affective state. These affective expectations are learned from prior experience and are automatically reproduced in the presence of stimuli similar to those present during the time of original learning. The discrepancy between the present and the anticipated affective states leads to approach or avoidance behaviour. The basic principle of affective arousal resulting out of discrepancies holds true even in case of an adult who has acquired (through learning) complex perceptual and cognitive processes.

It is to be emphasized that the redintegrated effect, according to the theory, involves a change in the present affective state of an organism at the time of arousal. A motive can not emerge independent of a change in affect, or in a situation which is incapable of producing a positive or negative affective change.

According to McClelland (1951) the achievement motive develops out of the expectations based on various experiences the individual has had with the common problems of life such as learning to walk, talk, eat by himself, fish, hunt, and learn a trade. In the process of mastering these problems, certain mastery cues (effort, difficulty, incompletion, etc.) will most probably get associated with affective arousal as resulting from reward or punishment and will come to evoke anticipation of success or failure on subsequent occasions. These associations may be strong or weak, depending upon the cultural differences in stress or early independence training or early achievement.

McClelland *et al.* (1953) also observed that motives can be measured effectively in imagination, in view of the fact that the behaviorual approach has been customarily utilized in order to measure "affect" of pleasure and pain. They distinguished between three aspects of motives' strength at the human level: dependability, intensity, and extensity. 'Motive dependability' or 'probability signifies that a motive will be aroused by a particular cue; 'Motive intensity' refers to the response amplitude in terms of latency or speed of response, and the number of responses per unit time: and 'motive extensity' indicates the pervasiveness of a motive or the variety of circumstances under which it will appear. 'Motive dependability' is the primary aspect of strength in that a motive must be first aroused before it can be measured in terms of intensity and extensity.

Achievement motive also known as 'need achievement (n-ach) or 'need mastery', is aroused by experimentally including ego-involvement. The concept of need for achievement was introduced by Murry (1938) which he described as the desire "to accomplish something difficult, to master, manipulate, or organize physical objects, human beings or ideas, to do this as rapidly, and as independently as possible, to excel oneself, to rival and surpass others, to increase self-regard by the successful exercise of talent". Sears (1942) linked n-Ach, a learned drive, to pride, craving, for superiority, ego-impulse, self-esteem, self-approval and self-assertion.

According to Cattell (1965), achievement motivation could be stated to spring from the three distinct dynamic sources, i.e., the self- sentiment, the super-ego, and the n-Ach construct which involves one's evaluations of his own performance according to a frame of reference or the criteria of good or bad performance. Such criteria signifying standards of excellence may be task related e.g., degree of perfection of performance) or self related (i.e., trying to improve upon the previous performance) or other related (i.e., social comparison competitive situations).

Academic Performance

An important aspect of the modern educational system is to find out the effectiveness and efficiency of teaching. This can be accomplished with the help of an evaluation system under which the performance of the students can be assessed. The present day educational institutions have therefore devised the examination system with the sole purpose of measuring the performance of students.

Academic performance is a part of the wider term educational growth. It refers to what a student has achieved in different subjects of studies during the course of the academic year. The academic performance can be viewed either from the perspective of inter-individual differences, that is, between one individual and another or intra-individual differences, that is , differences between one group of students and another. In the present study the analysis of data is confined to intra-individual differences as an attempt has been made to find out that how the academic performance levels of students belonging to different socio-economic categories vary from one another.

The concept of academic achievement or performance has been defined as a measure of a test as distinguished from aptitude and intelligence tests. The academic performance tests attempt to measure what has been accomplished by the students in various courses of studies, for example, Mathematics, History, Science and so on.

A number of scholars have defined the term academic achievement. Good (1959) defined academic achievement as, "the knowledge attained or skill developed in school subjects usually designated by test scores or marks assigned by the teacher."

Trow (1960) defined, "academic achievement as the attained ability or degree of competence in school task, usually measured by standardized tests and expressed in percentages or grade units based on norms derived from a wide sampling of pupils performance. In general, student's achievement means accomplishment or proficiency attained in an area of learning."

According to Carter (1940), "It is the common observation that success in academic achievement acts as an emotional tonic and any harm done to a child in the home or neighbourhood may be practically repaired by success in school or college. High achievement in school or college builds self-esteem and self-confidence which leads to better adjustment with other groups." In various reports of experiments conducted to test the importance of success of children indicated that the attainment of success causes children to set high and realistic goals for themselves. The importance of academic achievement can also be judged when we realize that fuller and happier life which we wish for every child would be impossible unless he had some skills in the intellectual and scholastic arts.

A number of researches have been conducted to find out the variables that promote achievement and those that are deterrent to it. Thus a number of variables - scholastic and personality, have been listed by the researchers which have been found to be associated with academic achievement. It is not possible to attribute the differences in academic performance to any single factor. Thus academic achievement is a multi-dimensional and multi-faceted phenomena. Dave (1960) reviewed seventeen studies on factors affecting academic achievement. He came to the conclusion that the various factors affecting the academic achievement can be genralised under two broad categories viz., personal and social factors. The personal factors can be further sub-divided into two types, that is cognitive and non-cognitive. The cognitive factors include intelligence, motivation, creativity and learning capacity. The non-cognitive factors include aptitude, level of aspiration, physical and mental health, self-concept of the learner and heredity. The social-factors include home or family environment, community, school environment, classroom environment, friends and socio-economic status. The factors mentioned above can affect academic performance both positively and adversely.

REVIEW OF LITERATURE

Some studies related with the conceptual and theoretical framework of achievement motivation and academic performance have already been discussed. In this section an attempt has been made to review some of the empirical studies with regard to the above mentioned topics. The empirical studies conducted in India as well as those conducted abroad have been taken into account.

A number of studies have been conducted to explore the relationship between achievement motivation and academic performance. Gupta (1986) found that there is a positive co-relation between achievement motivation and academic performance. Similar findings have been reported by Wilson (1993).

Lowell (1952) in his study related to achievement motivation and academic performance came to the conclusion that individuals who had higher levels of achievement motivation also depicted a higher level of performance in various courses of study especially in arithmetic and verbal skills.

McClelland *et al.* (1953) found that individuals who had high levels of achievement motivation were able to master problems on their own more often and earlier than those who had lower levels of academic achievement. These authors gathered data relating to the life histories and family background of children. They concluded that higher the achievement motivation scores of the sons, the more their parents tended to be seen (in terms of rating of parents by the subjects) as autocratic, rejecting, negligent and rigid.

A study was conducted by Atkinson (1953) regarding achievement motivation and the accomplishment of various tasks. The study concluded that there were no significant differences between high and low achievement motivation groups with reference to the completion of various tasks. However, there were significant differences in the recall of interrupted tasks in case of the two groups. According to him, the arousal of the tendency to approach success should be conceived as jointly determined by a disposition called the achievement motive and expectation that certain actions will lead to success.

Page (1958) conducted a study on the academic performance of school children. He came to the conclusion that those children who were given free comments (both praise and blame) about their performance on an objective test, achieved higher scores on subsequent tests.

Winterbotton (1958) conducted a study on the academic performance of the students and the attitudes of their mothers. The study concluded that the mothers whose sons had a higher level of achievement motivation expected the independence demands of their sons to be met at a particularly younger age as compared to the mothers whose sons had received lower achievement motivation scores.

Cox (1962) conducted a study on school children by using Thematic Appreciation Tests. He found that in case of young boys there was a significant relationship between achievement themes in the stories and the number of household duties and responsibilities which the child was reportedly entrusted with.

Lesser, Krawitz and Packard (1963) conducted a study related to achievement motivation among adolescent girls. They found that those female college students who had higher levels of achievement motivation showed arousal conditions only to the female pictures, whereas the females who had lower levels of achievement motivation showed such conditions with reference to the male pictures.

Rao (1965) conducted a study among students of M.S. University, Baroda in relation to some aspects of personality and academic adjustment among students. The study concluded that three independent variables – intelligence, study habits and school attitudes were significantly related to the scholastic achievement while the socio-economic status didnot have a significant relationship with scholastic achievement. Moreover, the academic achievement was significantly related with the intelligence level of the students.

Barial (1966) conducted a study on the educational achievement and motivation of school students. In this study an attempt was made to find out that how the social class background of the school students influence their achievement motivation and academic performance. The investigation revealed that there were no significant differences in the educational achievement, achievement motivation and intelligence level of the students belonging to various social classes. However, it was found that intelligence levels had a positive correlation with the scholastic achievement of the students.

Katz (1967) conducted a study regarding the socialization of academic motivation in minority group children. He found that the persons from low socio-economic group had a lower estimate of their achievement motivation and develop an avoidance reaction. He also maintained that the geographical environment is an important factor in determining the need to achieve. The persons facing hardships because of the geographical factor may tend to bear more risk and hence have higher levels of achievement motivation.

Heckhousen (1967) maintained that the relationship of achievement motivation with intelligence was bound to be different at different levels of intelligence. He further argued that a positive relationship between intelligence test performance and achievement motivation would be found among high ability subjects.

Shrivastava and Tiwari (1967) conducted a study on need achievement and related it to socio-economic stratification. They reported that the middle class had the highest level of need achievement. The high and the low socio-economic status groups differed significantly from the middle class in this context.

Dev Datta Sharma (1968) conducted a study among the students of Bhil tribe. The objective of the study was to examine the role played by education in the process of modernization of an educationally backward tribe. The study has described that how the spread of education has helped the tribal people to shift from tradition to modernity.

Maltesha (1969) conducted a study to examine the relationship between n-achievement, n-affiliation, n-power and socio-economic status. The study did not find any significant difference between lower and middle socio-economic groups with regard to need-achievement, need-affiliation and need-power.

Sharma and Singhal (1969) conducted a study to find out the relationship between parental occupation and school achievement. They found that the students belonging to high social class achieved slightly higher results as compared to those belonging to the middle class. However, the difference between the two social classes was not statistically significant. The students who belonged to high social class had better educational facilities and opportunities but middle class students seemed to makeup their deficiency to a large extent because they had a strong desire for personal achievement which was stronger as compared to the high social class boys.

Rabert, B. Fox (1969) studied the relationship between the low achievement motivation group and the high achievement motivation group with some variables like sex, achievement level, verbal intelligence, non-verbal intelligence, socio-economic status and level of educational aspirations. All the above mentioned relationships were found to be statistically significant.

Goswami (1969) has studied the role of school teachers in determining the educability. He examined the manner in which the role performance of the teacher affects the academic performance of the students.

Jerrath (1970) conducted a study related with personality co-relates of need achievement. The study revealed that there were no significant sex differences with respect to need achievement. The study demonstrated that the score of male and female subjects did not differ significantly in relation to need achievement and measures of personality. The second order factors of personality traits that is, anxiety and extraversion had some relationship with need achievement.

Gupta and Gupta (1970) conducted a study of anxiety and achievement motivation in relation to sex and socio-economic status. They found that anxiety and achievement motivation were negatively co-related for the group as a whole. Boys had a higher achievement motivation as compared to the girls. Moreover, those belonging to the middle socio-economic status had a higher level of achievement motivation than those who came either from upper or lower socio-economic status groups. The study concluded than an interaction of sex and socio-economic status is significant in producing differences in achievement motivation scores.

King (1970) conducted a study among students who were appearing for IIT entrance test. The study described the expectations, aspirations and motivations of the students appearing for a test for admission to IIT.

Choudhary (1971) used the TAT test prepared by Mehta (1969) for the assessment of achievement motivation and found that the girls received higher achievement motivation scores as compared to boys in Punjab.

Klinger (1971) conducted a study on achievement motivation and academic performance. He found that the respondents who received high n-Ach scores were extremely concerned with appearances, that is, with others' assessment of their performance. The implication is that the n-Ach scores reflect both intrinsic and extrinsic concerns.

Gokulnathan (1972) conducted a study among secondary school students of Assam. It was a comparative study of tribal and non-tribal students to find out their achievement motivation with reference to their racial, socio-cultural, educational and economic background. The findings of the study indicate that the tribal students, the girl students and those residing in rural areas received significantly higher n-Ach scores. The students whose fathers had middle or high educational status received high n-Ach scores as compared to the students whose fathers had low educational level. Moreover, students from middle and higher income groups had higher level of achievement motivation as compared to students belonging to the lower income groups.

De and Priya (1972) conducted a study which explored some personal and academic co-relates of achievement motivation. Dutt and Sabarwal (1973) also conducted a similar study among school students. Both these studies reported that the 'science' students had a significantly higher achievement motivation than 'arts' students. This might be explained with reference to the fact that science students are more hard working in nature and have a better perception of their goals. The quest for achieving the goals generates motivation in them as against 'arts' or 'commerce' students, only a few of whom know where they are heading for.

Kaur (1972) conducted a study on need achievement, study habits and socio-economic status of 10th class students in Patiala district of Punjab. The findings of the study reveal a higher n-Ach for female 10th class students than for male 10th class students. The study also reported a very high positive co-relation between n-Ach and study habits for urban boys. However, no significant co-relations were found between n-Ach and socio-economic status for any of the four groups that is, urban male, urban female, rural male and rural female.

Satpal Kaur (1973) conducted a study of need achievement in relation to personality adjustment of college students. The study indicated that the male students had higher need achievement than female students. However, no significant differences were found in the need achievement on the basis of residential background of students.

The Indian Council of Social Science Research (ICSSR) prepared an exhaustive survey of research in different fields of Sociology and Social Anthropology (1974). A trend report in the area of 'Sociology of Education' has been prepared by Suma Chitnis. This trend report identifies major areas and sub areas for research besides reviewing a large number of empirical studies in the field of Sociology of Education.

Thakur (1974) studied the academic achievement of high school boys. The study found that the boys with less aptitude for a particular subject failed to achieve satisfactorily in that subject. Those who had aptitude but disliked a subject did not show significant level of achievement motivation.

Pathak (1974) reported that the students belonging to high socio-economic status had more achievement motivation than those belonging to low socio-economic status. Similar findings have been reported by Dutt (1983).

Mubayi (1976) conducted a study of achievement motivation of secondary school students of scheduled tribes of South Gujrat. The study did not find any relation between educational level of fathers and n-Ach of students. Possibly students belonging to parents with high educational level tend to out do the educational attainments of their parents. On the other hand, students whose parents had low educational background are quite satisfied with their present educational attainment.

Gore (1977) has described the process of socialization among the Indian youth. He has focused on the outlook of students while presenting a conceptual framework regarding the socialization of Indian youth.

Reddy and Bhatt (1977) in their study of school youth have examined the aspiration of the top performers in post graduate examinations at the Punjab University, Chandigarh.

Patel (1977) conduced a study of achievement motivation, anxiety, performance at the university examination and socio-economic status of students in the colleges of education in the state of Gujrat. The study concluded that the higher economic group induces higher aspirations and motivates the children to identify themselves with and to internalise their parental status leading to higher achievement motivation.

Suma Chitnis (1977) in her study on education and equality has examined wastage, dropout and inequalities in enrolment in higher education among college students in

Bombay city. She has also probed intensively into the situation of these students and identified some of the problems encountered by them with a focus on understanding the differences between the situation of those who are at college in the city that are owned and conducted by the Peoples Education Society, especially established by Ambedkar for the educational advancement of the scheduled castes in Maharashtra and those who are enrolled at other colleges owned and conducted by the government or by other private managements.

Singh and Kumar (1977) conducted a study which examined the relationship of need achievement with personality groups. The study found that the male and female post graduate students did not differ from one another with respect to need achievement. The study also reported that the need achievement and extraversion among post graduate male and female students are highly co-related.

Clarence (1978) conducted a study on the effect of achievement motivation and socio-economic background on the earnings of young men. He found that, achievement motivation is an important determinant of individual earnings and a possible vehicle for the intergenerational transfer of economic inequality. Moreover, socio-economic background differences are significant factors in explaining learning differences both directly and indirectly.

Abbasayulu (1978) studied the impact of higher education among the scheduled caste, scheduled tribe and backward class students in Osmania University Jurisdiction. He refers to the changes brought about by education in these weaker sections of the Indian society. He also refers to the apathy of tribal students towards education.

Yadav (1979) compared the intelligence level and motivational tendencies of scheduled caste and non-scheduled caste students. The study included fifty students from each of these groups. The study concluded that there were no significant differences between scheduled caste and non-scheduled caste students both with respect to intelligence as well as motivational levels.

McGill (1979) conducted a study on test performance as a function of socio-economic status. He found that within the overall fourth grade student population of 515, low socio-economic status students obtained significantly lower average achievement motivation scores as compared to middle socio-economic status students. The comparisons of reading comprehension scores of low and middle socio-economic status groups indicated that the low SES students obtained significantly lower scores and that within each SES group low n-Ach students obtained lower reading comprehension scores. When SES groups were equated with respect to n-Ach students obtained lower reading comprehension scores. When SES groups were equated with respect to n-Ach and retested under tangible or intangible reward conditions, SES differences in reading comprehension scores persisted, substantially favouring middle SES students. The results of the study suggested that standardized test performance differences between low and middle SES students cannot be directly attributed to differences in achievement motivation levels.

Chitnis (1981) authored a National report on a survey of scheduled caste high school and college students in fifteen states of India. The study involved several social scientists and aimed at collecting some basic data concerning the situation and the problems of scheduled caste and scheduled tribe school and college students in the country. The reports on individual states are available either in publications or in mimeographs authored by the scholars who were responsible for the study in different states. The statistical tables compiled by V.P. Shah have also been published.

Aggarwal and Suraksha (1981) conducted a study on achievement motivation at high and low levels of perception of personal control. The study found that high interval group had significantly higher achievement motivation than the low interval group. However, there was no significant difference in the strength of achievement motive of high socio-economic status group. The study also revealed that the boys exhibited a stronger achievement motive than girls.

Chauhan (1982) conducted a study of academic motivation in relation to intelligence and socio-economic status. The study reported that academic motivation of girls in general is lower than the average academic motivation of boys. The study also concluded that academic motivation is highly correlated with intelligence.

Ismail (1982) conducted a study of relationship between achievement motivation and learning styles of a group of Malaysia students attending Northern Illinois University. The study concluded that:

(a) The motive to avoid failure was related to concrete learning.

(b) The motive to achieve success was related to abstract learning.

(c) Academic group and the level of schooling were significant factors in correlating achievement motivation with learning styles.

(d) Achievement motivation was found to be independent of dominant learning style preference.

Kamala (1983) conducted a study on achievement motivation in relation to masculinity-feminity. The study found that significant differences exist between high masculine and low masculine subjects with respect to achievement motivation. Moreover, the relationship between achievement motivation and masculinity-feminity are significant even when the effect of intelligence and socio-economic status are partialled out separately and in combination.

Donals (1983) conducted a study on achievement motivation as a factor related to the diagnostic problem solving effectiveness of students of automotive technology. The study found that the group which was highest in achievement motivation was found to be superior to the group which was lowest in achievement motivation with respect to problem solving knowledge.

Jyothi (1984) conducted a study of achievement motivation in relation to personality dimension and performance among high and low achieving girl students. The study found a positive relationship between achievement motive and personality. Significant differences were found in the personality dimension of low and high achievers. However, with regard to academic performance the differences were not significant.

Kiran and Singh (1984) conducted a study on the effect of parental education, economic status and academic stream on the achievement motivation. The study found that the students belonging to high parental education group had significantly higher achievement motivation scores as compared to those belonging to the low parental education group. The science students had a significantly higher achievement motivation scores as compared to arts and commerce students who did not differ significantly from each other as far as achievement motivation scores are concerned.

Pathak and Shukla (1985) carried out a study of aspirations and achievement motivation of scheduled caste students – teachers. They found that students-teachers from scheduled castes recognise the help of the government and society and have a desire to achieve high status. It was also found that their need for achievement is not less than that of the upper caste students or teachers.

Sandhu (1985) conducted a study of need achievement among rural and urban school students in relation to certain socio-economic variables and sex. The study found that:

(a) there were no significant sex differences in need achievement among the rural and urban school students;

(b) there were no significant sex differences in the socio-economic variables of rural and urban school students;

(c) there were significant differences of need-achievement on the basis of three levels of socio-economic status;

(d) there were no interactional effects of sex and school background, sex and SES, school background and SES on n-Ach of 10th class students.

Sontakey (1986) carried out a comparative study of personality factors and achievement motivation of high and low achievers in natural and biological sciences. The study found that the high achievers were more intelligent than the low achievers. The high achievers also belonged to a higher socio-economic status background.

Gupta (1989) conducted a study of school boys and girls in relation to their achievement motivation and academic performance. 310 boys and 312 girls were given achievement motivation test. The study showed that the girls had greater achievement motivation and higher academic achievement motivation than boys.

Mamta Sharma (1992) conducted a study on the impact of preferred music on academic performance of students. The study found significant differences in the academic performance of the music and the non-music groups. The study also found that the physiological and psychological responses were affected by preferred music.

Kaur (1993) conducted a study on the vocational interests of school students in relation to their intelligence and academic achievement. The study found that:

(a) there were no significant differences between male and female school students with regard to intelligence;

(b) there were no significant differences between male and female school students on academic achievement;

(c) there was significant difference between rural and urban students with respect to intelligence. The urban students were more intelligent than the rural students;

(d) there were no significant differences between rural and urban students and their academic achievement.

Patil *et al.* (1994) examined the influence of self-concept and achievement motivation on sex role perception of 360 adolescent boys and girls. The objective of the study was to find out the influence of self-concept and achievement motivation on boys and girls. It is evident from the results that the adolescent who had high achievement motivation were more liberal in sex role perception. Those who had low achievement motivation were more conservative in sex role perception. The mean scores of sex role perception also revealed the same results.

Dewan (1996) conducted a comparative study of academic achievement, family environment, classroom environment, achievement motivation and intelligence of senior secondary students of different socio-economic groups. The major conclusions of the study were that:

(a) the boys and girls had significant differences with regard to academic achievement, family and classroom environment, achievement motivation, SES and intelligence;

(b) It was observed that girls had higher academic achievement, perceived family and classroom environment in a better manner than boys, had higher achievement motivation and intelligence.

Krishnamurthy (2001) concluded a study about achievement as related to academic achievement motivation and attitude towards study of history. Data were collected from 455 students selected by using the cluster sampling technique consisting of 222 urban and 233 rural students. Finding of study reveals that 54.5% of students have relatively high level of academic achievement motivation and rest 45.5 % have relatively low level.

Koteswara and Reddy (2001) conducted a comparative study of the characteristics of high and low achievers in reading of class 8th pupils with special reference to school and home factors. The study was conducted among school students of Andhra Pardesh. The study described the impact of fourteen personality factors on achievement motivation. It was found that all the fourteen factors had a significant influence on reading achievement of high school students. The students whose personality characteristics were out-going, more intelligent, emotionally stable, excitable and assertive performed significantly better than students whose personality characteristics were classified as less intelligent, shy, tough minded, undisciplined and relaxed.

Naik, A.K. (2002) conducted a study to explore the place of motivation in learning. The aim of the study was to understand how low 'motivation' affects learning. The study concluded that it is the responsibility of the teacher to promote interest in children with regard to learning. Learning will proceed best if motivated by teachers. So in order to make teaching learning process effective a teacher can use some motivational techniques for achievement.

Dutt, Sunil and Kumar, Devinder (2002) conducted a study on secondary school students. The study analysed the effectiveness on achievement in Economics in relation to cognitive style of senior secondary school students. A sample of 400 students studying in 10+2 class was selected randomly from seven schools of Ambala district and significant differences were found in the levels of achievement motivation. Field independence-dependence cognitive style did not bring any differential achievement in Economics.

Meenakshi (2003) had made an in-depth study of the different subjects of study in the aggregate in the matriculation. Annual examination conducted by P.S.E.B in March-April (2003) of boys and girls of all districts. From this study, we come to know that Mathematics has been causality. Government school shows a very poor performance of 47% pass. Some consistent efforts have to be made to strengthen the teaching of this subject in secondary school.

Geeta Devi (2003) has reported positive and significant relation of intelligence with math's and language achievement of secondary school students. She also found that though thee was no significant gender difference in intelligence. Boys had higher mean score in math's then girls. Where as girls were better achievers in language.

Shan (2003) has reported that only double talented high school girls (high on intelligence and creativity) have significantly higher levels of academic achievement.

Singh and Kaur (2003) investigated that achievement motivation and parental background as determinants of students academic achievement. The objectives of this study are:

(i) to find out the relationships between students academic achievement and their achievement motivation; and

(ii) to find out the effect of working of parents on students.

It was found that there is a positive correlation between achievement motivation and academic achievement of students. Qualifications of parents and working of parents does not show significant effect on student achievement motivation and academic achievement. The result also showed that children of service group were found to have significantly better achievement motivation as compared to their counter parts.

Aggarwal and Singh (2004) studied achievement motivation of co-educational and single sex educational secondary students. The objective of the study was to find out the level of achievement motivation among students of co-education and single sex schools. The study revealed that boys of co-education institution were found having more achievement motivation than the students of single sex institution where as girls were found having no impact of kind of institutions on their achievement motivation.

Kaur (2004) compared achievement motivation of rural and urban students. The objective of the study was to find out the difference between boys and girls on achievement motivation. The results showed that there was significant difference between achievement motivation of boys and girls. Mean scores of girls of achievement motivation test were 35.32 which was greater than mean scores of boys i.e. 34.57. The finding of the study also showed insignificant difference between achievement motivation of urban and rural students.

Gakhar (2004) studied the acquisition of geographical concepts in relation to intelligence, socio-economic and personality variables. The present study was conducted on random sample of Xth class 300 students (both boys and girls) taken from six senior secondary schools of Ferozpur district of Punjab. The objective of the study was to find out the correlation between intelligence, socio-economic status, personality and geographical concepts. Results revealed significant correlation of intelligence, socio-economic status, personality factor A, B, C, G, 1 and Q2 with the acquisition of geographical concepts.

Kaur *et al.* (2004) studied intellectual and non intellectual correlates of scientific attitude of 740 students of government and non-government schools of Punjab. The objective of the study was to find out the relationship between intelligence and scientific attitude of students. Results showed that level of intelligence and scientific attitude of students had positive and significant relationships.

Begum and Phukan (2005) investigated correlation between academic achievement and intelligence. The sample consists of 180 students of class 9th out of which 118 were male and 62 female students. The results revealed that intelligence of students under the study were positively correlated (0.70) with academic achievement.

Pathania and Kaur (2005) reported that the present study was undertaken with the objective of assessing the problems faced by tribal adolescents of Himachal Pradesh in getting education. The findings of the present study also showed that the respondents of selected districts perceived home, school, personal and community constraints more than the other districts and were significantly different from other communities. Non-significant differences were observed in the perception of constraints among high, medium and low income group respondents, except in the teacher's behaviour, stress and fear experienced at school.

Colman (2005) concluded that achievement motivation s n-Ach a social form of motivation involving a competitive drive to meet standards of excellence Achievement motivation is an essential element which effect the behaviour of all members.

Sharma *et al.* (2006) investigated the Relationships between Self-Concept, Achievement Motivation and Achievement in Mathematics; A Gender Comparison. The investigator concluded that here is no significant relationship between self-concept and achievement motivation of boys but there is significant positive relationships between self-concept and achievement in mathematics.

Sachdeva (2006) opined that occurrences of a problem in the classroom is a natural phenomenon as there are many students coming from different socio-economic strata of life.

Allwords Dictionary (2006) stated that intelligence in the ability to use memory, knowledge, experience, understanding, reasoning, imagination and judgment in order to solve problems and adopt to new situations.

Vaidya, P.M. and Mulgaonkar, K.P. (2007) found that students can learn to overcome anxiety by applying or using strategy which simply involves practice with math problems with students who have the highest expectancies for future success. (and the highest self efficiency are the one's who attribute their successes to stable and dependable factor such as high innate ability) and, inturn, also have higher achievement.

OBJECTIVES OF THE STUDY

(i) To classify rural and urban college students with reference to various levels of achievement motivation and academic performance.

(ii) To find out the relationship of social factors (Caste, educational level of family, type of family and place of residence), with achievement motivation and academic performance of the college students.

(iii) To explore the relationship of economic factors (occupational structure and income level of family) with achievement motivation and academic performance.

(iv) To find out the reasons for variations in the levels of academic performance of the students.

HYPOTHESES

The following null hypotheses have been put to test in the present study.

1. There will be no significant difference in the need achievement and academic performance of rural and urban students.
2. There will be no gender differences in the need achievement and academic performance of college students.

3. There will be no difference with regard to the impact of socio-economic status on need achievement and academic performance.
4. There might not be significant differences in the levels of achievement motivations of arts and commerce students.
5. The educational levels of the respondents' families might not have a significant influence on academic performance and level of achievement motivation.

METHODOLOGY

Research in any field means an intensive, purposeful and systematic search for knowledge and understanding of social or physical phenomena. As stated in the *Encyclopaedia of Social Sciences*, "social research is a systematic method of exploring, analyzing and conceptualizing social life in order to extend, correct or verify knowledge, it aids in construction of a theory or in the practice of an art." The purpose of research is to discover answers to questions through the application of scientific procedure that is, research methods. During the last two decades, the methodology has come to occupy an increasingly important place in social research. Methodology can be considered as the application of fundamentals of science to the field of sociology.

Research is carried through a certain procedure called a design. The Macmillian Dictionary of Sociology states that, "research design is a broad plan of a piece of empirical research, specifying the manner in which the data is to be collected and analyzed in order to test hypotheses derived from a theory or to develop insights into the problems being investigated in a manner that aims to combine relevance to the research purpose with economy of the research."

The present study has been undertaken to describe the levels of achievement motivation and academic performance of rural and urban college students, and relate them to socio-economic variables. The research work, therefore, employs a descriptive research design. The data have been collected through structured interview schedule which included achievement motivation scales, details about socio-economic background of respondents and their academic performance.

Keeping in view the nature and the objectives of the present study different aspects of methodology can be described under following headings:

1. Locale of the study.
2. Selection of respondents.
3. Tools of enquiry.
4. Collection of data.
5. Tabulation, analysis and interpretation of data.

LOCALE OF THE STUDY

For the present study Patiala district of Punjab has been selected purposively, mainly due to convenience as well as the time and financial constraints of the researcher. One rural and one urban college from Patiala district of Punjab has been selected randomly from the lists of colleges. These lists were procured from the Punjabi University office. The lists of students were procured from the selected colleges and proportional random sample was drawn from among the male and female students. Multani Mal Degree college was selected from Patiala city and Government College from Dera Bassi (Rural College)

SELECTION OF THE RESPONDENTS

For the collection of data, a random sample of 25 students each from arts and commerce streams was drawn from each college. The sample consisted of B.A. and B.Com first, second and final year students. Equal number of males and females were included in the sample. Thus, the total sample size was 300 respondents. The selected respondents were interviewed with the help of a structured interview schedule.

TOOLS OF ENQUIRY

The important techniques of fieldwork, which have been used by the researcher include observation and interview schedule . In order to facilitate the research work it was decided to combine the interview technique with that of structured schedule.

First of all, the available studies concerning the research problem were studied as it enabled the investigator to have an insight into the problem that was most helpful in framing the interview schedule. In order to get reliable information regarding the problem, suitable questions were framed. A structured interview schedule was prepared keeping in mind the objectives of study. It was pre-tested and finalized after making necessary modifications.

The interview schedule includes questions pertaining to the socio-economic background of the respondents, their academic performance and motivational level. In accordance with the major objectives of the present research, Asha Bhatnagar's scale was used for arriving at the achievement motivation levels of the respondents. The various statements for the construction of the scale were included in the interview schedule. The responses to these statements were assigned scores and depending on the total scores received by the respondents, they were classified into three categories of achievement motivation, that is, low, medium and high. The interview schedule also included questions regarding academic performance of the respondents.

COLLECTION OF DATA

The authors herself collected the primary data. All the respondents were interviewed with the help of a structured interview schedule. Special care was taken that only reliable and valid information should be noted down in the schedules. Editing of the schedules was done to check any discrepancies in the data.

The interview went on for long hours because the respondents had to give complete information about their social life, about their studies and had to respond to various statements related to achievement motivation and academic performance. Firstly, students were not ready to give the required information, but when they were explained about the purpose of the study and about confidentiality of the information provided by them, they were ready to co-operate. A number of students hesitated to give information about the income of their parents/guardians as they were not sure about the exact income. They were therefore asked to tell the approximate income of their parents/guardians.

TABULATION AND ANALYSIS OF DATA

First of all, the relevant information received from the structured interview schedules was coded with the help of a code design. After giving code numbers to the data, all the relevant data was tabulated on data sheets and was computerized.

Frequency distribution and percentages were calculated and cross tabulation was done with the help of statistical techniques.

CHAPTER - II

SOCIO-ECONOMIC PROFILE OF THE RESPONDENTS

In social science research it is important to describe the socio-economic characteristics of the respondents as they have an important bearing on the individuals attitudes, behaviour and activities. People belonging to different social and economic background are likely to perceive various social aspects differently and their behaviour is bound to be different. The background information of the respondents is essential for the further analysis of data which is presented in the ensuing chapters. Thus, it will be worthwhile to have some knowledge about the socio-economic background and demographic characteristics of the respondents prior to the analysis of their responses. The following special characteristics of the respondents have been described in this chapter - age, caste, religion gender, college in which studying rural-urban background, educational score of the family, income of the family, family type and occupation of the parent/guardian.

RELIGION

The attitudes, beliefs and action patterns of an individual are deeply influenced by the religion to which he/she is affiliated. The State of Punjab has faced many changes from the religious point of view. Under the influence of Sikhism, many Hindu families converted to Sikh religion but retained their caste affiliations. That is why one can find a number of caste groups in Punjab which are common both among Hindus and Sikhs. Thus, Hindus and Sikhs are the two major religious groups of Panjab.

After partition of the country some of the Muslim families did not migrate to Pakistan and remained in India. Thus, one can also find a few Muslim families in Panjab. The distribution of respondents in different religious categories has been shown in Table 2.1.

Table 2.1: Distribution of the respondents according to their religious affiliation

Religion	Frequency	Percentage
Sikh	106	35. 33
Hindu	189	63.00
Muslim	5	1.67
Total	**300**	**100.00**

The data presented in the preceding table show that a majority of respondents (63%) belonged to Hindu religion followed by Sikhs (35.33%). There were only five Muslim families in the sample.

CASTE BACKGROUND

The caste system is a very deep rooted and all powerful institution in the Indian society. It has a significant impact on all other institutions-economic, political, religious and educational. As caste system is so powerful in all aspects of life, it was considered essential together information about the caste background of the respondents. This information was necessary because one of the hypotheses of the present study is that caste background of an individual is likely to influence his/her academic performance and level of achievement motivation. In the present study there were five

Muslim households who didn't mention any caste. Therefore, the caste analysis has been confined to Hindu and Sikh families. The respondents had mentioned various caste groups. For the purpose of analysis these caste groups have been classified into three categories, that is high, medium and low castes. Jats and Brhmins were placed in the high caste category. Khatris, Banias and artisan castes were included in the medium caste category and backward and scheduled castes were placed in the low caste category. Brahmins were included in the high caste category as they are traditionally considered ritually superior to other caste groups. Jats have also been included in the high status category because they are the dominant caste group in Punjab due to their numerical as well as economic strength. Khatris, Banias and artisan castes have been included in the medium status category of caste because these caste groups, though not ritually very high, still pursue occupations which are not considered 'unclean' or 'defiling'. The backward and the scheduled caste have been included in the low status category because in the traditional caste system they were assigned a low status because of their degrading occupations which were considered as impure, as well as low economic status. The five Muslim families were excluded from the analysis of caste. The distribution of respondents in these caste categories has been presented in Table 2.2.

Table 2.2: Distribution of respondents according to their caste categories

Caste categories	Frequency	Percentage
High	60	20.34
Medium	157	53.22
Low	78	26.44
Total	**295**	**100.00**

* The five Muslim families have been excluded from the analysis.

The foregoing table indicates that the highest proportion of the respondents (53.22%) were placed in the medium caste category, followed by 26.44% in the low caste category and

20.34% in the high caste category. The caste background of the respondents was cross-tabulated with their place of residence and the analysis of data in this context has been presented in Table 2.3.

Table 2.3: Distribution of respondents according to their caste categories and place of residence

Caste categories	Place of residence		
	Rural	Urban	Total
High	25 (41.67%)	35 (58.33%)	60
Medium	69 (43.95%)	88 (56.05%)	157
Low	52 (66.67%)	26 (33.33%)	78
Total	**146**	**149**	**295**

The data presented in the foregoing table indicate that two-thirds of the low caste respondents were residing in the rural areas. On the other hand, a majority of the high and medium caste respondents were residing in the urban areas.

FAMILY TYPE

The type of family in which an individual lives has significant influence on his personal and social life. Family is the most important institution in the socialization process of the individual. Moreover, the family ascribes an initial status to the individual prior to his achieving status on his own. In India one can find various types of families. However, for the present study the classification of families given by Morrison (1959) has been employed. The classification of family types into three major categories i.e., the nuclear quasi-joint and the joint has been done by Morrison, by taking the conjugal pair as a basic unit. Accordingly, the nuclear family consists of one conjugal pair with or without other relatives and the joint family consists of two or more conjugal pairs with or without other relatives. If the joint family consists of only two conjugal pairs with or without other relatives and further if the husbands in the two pairs are related as father and son, this type of family has been termed as quasi-joint by Morrison.

The classification of Morrison has been adopted in the present study because of its suitability for empirical research. The distribution of these three types of families in the sample of the present study has been depicted in Table 2.3. In all these types of families co-residence and commensality of the members are assumed. Table 2.4 shows the distribution of respondents according to their family type categories.

Table 2.4: Distribution of the respondents according to their family types

Family Type	Frequency	Percentage
Nuclear family	187	62.33
Joint family	90	30.00
Quasi-Joint family	23	7.67
Total	**300**	**100.00**

The data presented in the above table indicate that the maximum number of respondents belonged to the nuclear families, that is, 62.33% followed by those who were living in joint families (30%). Very few respondents (7.67%) belonged to quasi joint families.

EDUCATIONAL SCORE OF THE FAMILY

The educational level of a family is believed to have a profound influence on the attitudes and behaviour of its members. Some studies reviewed in the previous chapter have also demonstrated that the educational level of the family has an important bearing on the level of achievement motivation and academic performance of its members. The educational score of the family can also be a good indicator regarding the general socio-economic standing of the family in the community. Accordingly, it was decided to assign educational scores to each family with reference to number of educated persons in the family and the level of their education. Thus, a score of one was assigned to those who had studied upto matriculation, score of two to those who had studied up to graduation and a score of three to those who had studied up to post-graduation or some professional course of post-graduate level. The total educational score was worked out for each family and depending on the range of scores, the families were classified into low, medium and high categories. The families whose total educational score was up to 4, were placed in the low category; families receiving scores between 4 and 8 were placed in the medium category and the families obtaining more than 8 scores were included in the high category. Table 2.5 shows the distribution of the families according to their educational score categories.

Table 2.5: Distribution of the respondents according to the educational score categories of their families

Educational Score Categories	Frequency	Percentage
Low Score	22	7.33
Medium Score	151	50.33
High Score	127	42.33
Total	**300**	**100.00**

The data given in the above table reveals that the highest proportion of the families (50.33%) were placed in the medium score category, followed by 42.33% in the high score category. Very few families that is, 7.33% had received low educational scores.

In order to compare the educational scores of rural and urban families, the analysis was carried further. The distribution of rural and urban families according to their educational scores has been presented in Table 2.6.

Table 2.6: Distribution of rural and urban families according to their educational scores

Educational Score Categories	Rural area		Urban area		Total	
	F	%	F	%	F	%
Low Score	16	10.67	6	4.00	22	7.33
Medium Score	91	60.67	60	40.00	151	50.33
High Score	43	28.67	84	56.00	127	42.33
Total	**150**	**100.00**	**150**	**100.00**	**300**	**100.00**

$\chi^2 = 24.146$; df = 2; $p > 0.1$

The foregoing table reveals that a very high proportion of the urban families had received high educational scores as compared to the rural families. Whereas only 28.67% of the rural families were placed in the high educational score category, the corresponding percentage for the urban families was 56%, which is double than that of the rural families. This shows a greater prevalence of higher education in the urban families as compared to the rural families. The Chi-square (χ^2) test also depicts a significant association between these two variables, that is, rural-urban residence and educational scores of the families.

The educational scores of the family were co-related with the occupation of parents/guardians of the respondents and the analysis of data in this context has been presented in the Table 2.7.

The analysis of data presented in the table depict that none of the families which had received educational scores was engaged in high status job. On the other hand about three-fourth of the parents/guardians who were in high status jobs belonged to families with high educational scores. Very few agricultural families (3.15%) had received high educational scores (Table 2.7).

Table 2.7: Distribution of families according to their educational scores and occupation of parents/ guardians

Educational scores of the family	Occupation of Parents/Guardians				
	Jobs (H)	Jobs (L)	Business	Agriculture	Total
Low	–	7 (31.82%)	5 (22.73%)	10 (45.45%)	22
Medium	10 (6.62%)	75 (49.67%)	49 (32.45%)	17 (11.26%)	151
High	31 (24.41%)	45 (37.19%)	47 (38.84%)	4 (3.15%)	127
Total	**41**	**127**	**101**	**31**	**300**

AGE

Age is an important factor in influencing an individual's psychological and social perceptions. The respondents of the present study were the college students and hence all of them were young in age. Accordingly they have been divided in two age categories, i.e., non-adult (upto 18 years.) and adults (above 18 years). Their distribution in these age catagories has been presented in Table 2.8.

Table 2.8: Distribution of the respondents according to their age categories

Age Categories	Frequency	Percentage
Upto 18 years	117	39.00
Above 18 years	183	61.00
Total	**300**	**100.00**

The table given above shows that a majority of the respondents (61%) were adults that is, above 18 years of age. The remaining (39%) respondents had not yet become adults as they were below 18 years of age.

GENDER

Gender refers to the fact whether a person is male or female. Most people assume that masculinity and feminity have standardized meaning. However, what is desirable in a man or a woman differs significantly from time to time and from society to society. The cultural perceptions linked with gender determine the varying roles of males and females in a society. The process of socialization also leads to different patterns of thinking and behaviour among the two genders. Thus one can expect different types of responses from male and female respondents. An effort was made by the present researcher to include an equal number of males and females in the sample. However due to lesser number of girl students in some classes there has been a slender difference in the number of male and female respondents Thus 153 males (51%) and 147 females (49%) constituted the sample of the present study.

COLLEGE OF RESPONDENTS

One of the major objectives of the present study is to compare the students from rural and urban colleges with regard to their achievement motivation and academic performance. In order to meet this objective the lists of rural and urban colleges affiliated to Punjabi University, Patiala were procured from the university office. One college each from rural and urban colleges was selected randomly. Both the selected colleges were coeducational. It was considered essential to select equal number of students from both the colleges to facilitate comparison between them. Multani Mal Degree College was selected from Patiala city (urban college) and Government College was selected from Dera Bassi (rural college). An equal number of students that is, 150 each was selected from both the colleges for the purpose of the present study.

RURAL URBAN BACKGROUND

It is generally believed that the area of residence exercises a significant influence on the attitudes and behaviour of the people. Accordingly, it was decided to include an equal number of respondents from rural and urban areas in the sample. The inclusion of equal number of students from these two types of areas will be useful in comparing the levels of achievement motivation and academic performance of the students from these two types of areas.

FIELD OF STUDY

For the purpose of present research work the students have been selected from two fields of study, that is, arts and commerce. The science students could not be included in the sample because the science courses were not being offered in any of the rural colleges. Accordingly it was decided to confine the sample of the present research work only to the above mentioned two fields of study. There are three classes in the arts stream, that is, B.A. I, II, and III. Similarly, there were three classes in the commerce stream, that is, B.Com I, II and III. It was considered appropriate to include an equal number of students from each of the six classes. Thus, fifty students each were selected from every class leading to total sample of 300 respondents. Moreover, an equal number of students was included in the sample from the rural and urban colleges. Thus twenty five students each were included in the sample from the six classes from both rural and urban colleges.

OCCUPATION OF PARENTS/GUARDIANS

An occupation can be described as a particular action or course of action in which one is engaged especially; habitually to earn one's living. Sociologically it may be designated as a specific activity having value, which enables an individual to obtain a steady flow of income. Occupation is one of the social determinants of one's economic status and it affects the life style, behaviour and one's role in the society.

The respondents of the present study were asked to mention the occupation of their parent/guardian. A large number of occupations were mentioned by the respondents. Thus it was necessary to classify various occupations in some categories for the purpose of further statistical analysis. The various occupations have been categorised into four categories, that is, high status jobs, low status jobs, business and agriculture. The classification in the low status and high status occupations was done with reference to the income level. The persons having a monthly income upto Rs. 5,000 were placed in the low status category of occupations and those having incomes above Rs. 5,000 per month were included in the high satus category. The distribution in these occupational categories has been presented in Table 2.9.

Table 2.9: Distribution of respondents according to their parents/guardians occupation

Parent's/guardian's Occupation	Frequency	Percentage
High Status jobs	41	13.67
Low status jobs	127	42.33
Business	101	33.67
Agriculture	31	10.33
Total	**300**	**100.00**

The preceding table shows that the highest proportion of parents/guardians of the respondents (42.33%) were engaged in low status jobs, followed by those who were engaged in business (33.67%). Very few of them were engaged in high status jobs (13.67%) and agriculture (10.33%).

PARENTS/GUARDIAN'S INCOME

Income is considered to be the most important variable in determining the socio-economic status of an individual. The income of an individual also influences the quality of life. The respondents of the present study were students and therefore had no income of their own. Therefore the income of their parents/guardians has been taken into consideration because this has a direct bearing on the life of the students. The parents/guardian's of the respondents have been divided in three categories of monthly income, that is, upto Rs. 5,000 (low income group); between Rs. 5,001-10,000 (middle income group);

and above Rs. 10,000 (high income group). The distribution of the parent's/guardians in these income categories has been shown in Table 2.10.

Table 2.10: Distribution of respondents parents/guardians of the respondents in monthly income categories

Monthly Income (in Rupees)	Frequency	Percentage
Upto 5,000	108	36.00
5001-10,000	131	43.67
Above 10,001	61	20.33
Total	**300**	**100.00**

The table given above indicates that a higher proportion of parents/guardian's were placed in the middle income category of Rs. 5,001-10,000 (43.67%). Another 36% were in the category of upto Rs. 5000, that is, the lower income category. About one-fifth (20.33%) were placed in the high income category of above Rs. 10,000.

The analysis was carried further to find out the pattern of income distribution in the rural and urban areas. The analysis in this context is presented in Table 2.11.

Table 2.11: Distribution of Parents/guardians in income categories and place of residence

Income Categories	Rural		Urban		Total	
	F	%	F	%	F	%
Upto 5000	86	57.33	22	14.67	108	36.00
5001-10,000	54	36.00	77	51.33	131	43.67
Above-10,000	10	6.67	51	34.00	61	61.33
Total	**150**	**100.00**	**150**	**100.00**	**300**	**100.00**

$\chi^2 = 69.521$ df = 2 p> 0.1

The foregoing table indicates that a majority of the rural residents (57.33%) were placed in the lower income category while a majority of the urban residents (51.33%) were placed in the middle income category. The analysis also revealed that a much higher proportion of urban residents (34%) were placed in the high income category while the corresponding percentage for the rural residents was only 6.67%. Thus the analysis shows that the urban residents were economically more well-off as compared to the rural residents.

❑ ❑ ❑ ❑ ❑

CHAPTER - III

SOCIAL FACTORS AFFECTING ACHIEVEMENT MOTIVATION

All types of human behaviour is based on some or the other cause. The prime causations of behaviour are motives. Motives play a major role and are the causative factors of human behaviour. When a person tries to manifest concern for excellence in his work, we refer to it as behaviour backed by achievement motive.

According to Skinner "Motivation is a general term that encompasses those states of the individual under which he attends to certain aspects of his environment. As a result his behaviour is both initiated and directed."

Atkinson (1964) states that the theory of achievement motivation attempts to account for the determinants of the direction, magnitude and persistence of behaviour in limited but very important domain of human activities.

Besides its general significance, the importance and the need of study of motivation construct in the educational and academic field is being increasingly realized. One of the most baffling and perplexing problems faced by modern psychologists and educationists is to identify those personality factors which determine academic success at the school or the college level. On the basis of extensive review of research, Crandall (1963) has stated that research in child psychology concerning achievement as a dispositional system as compared to other areas is still at a premature level. Whereas research pertaining to achievement and abilities has been conducted for a long time, investigations into the motivational components of child's achievement are still at an incipient stage.

Achievement motivation, also referred to as the need for achievement (and abbreviated n-achievement), is a wish to do well. It refers to the behaviour of an individual who strives to accomplish something, to do his best to excel others in performance. This involves competition for a particular standard of excellence of performance.

The concept of achievement motivation was put forth by Murry (1938), but it is through the hard labour of McClelland and his co-workers that this aspect has assumed practical importance in education and other fields. It has been well recognized by psychologists that achievement motivation is a specific personality dimension. A study of possible relationship between achievement motivation and academic performance has remained a topic of great concern for psychologists. It is regarded as a determinant of an individual's as well as nation's achievement in various fields. McClelland's (1961), study of its relationship to entrepreneurial behaviour has indicated that economic growth in any society is dependent on the existence of a high level of need for achievement among people in that society.

McClelland (*ibid*) defined achievement motivation in terms of effect in connection with evaluated performance in which "competition with a standard of excellence" was parmount. This affect is seen as reflecting at least two components "hope and success" and "fear of failure."

Alderman (1974) stated that achievement motivation is related to the achievement oriented performances, situations in which the person know that he will be evaluated, that competition will be present, that there will be some risk to the outcome, that the outcome will be either favourable or unfavourable to him, and the excellence of his performance will be judged.

A number of scales have been developed by scholars to measure levels of achievement motivation among individuals. In the present study the scale developed by Asha Bhatnagar (1999) has been used. In Bhatnagar's scale 40 statements have been included which are related to achievement motivation and academic performance of the students. The respondents were asked to read each statement carefully, think about them and then respond to each statement in any of the alternatives, that is 'yes', 'undecided' and 'no' cells against each statement. There was no time limit for completing the inventory but respondents were asked to finish it as quickly as possible. They were also requested to give their responses sincerely and without any hesitation.

The statements were of two types, that is, positive and negative. For the positive statements 'yes' was given two scores, 'undecided' one and 'No' was given zero score. On the other hand, in case of the negative statements 'No' was given two scores, 'undecided' One and 'Yes' zero score. The scores received by each respondent were added and according to the range of scores, the respondents were divided into three categories, that is, low, medium and high. The distribution of respondents in these categories has been presented in Table 3.1.

Table 3.1: Distribution of Respondents According to Achievement Motivation Score Categories

Categories	Frequency	Percentage
Low	38	12.67
Medium	203	67.67
High	59	19.67
Total	**300**	**100.00**

The data presented in Table 3.1 indicate that two-thirds of the respondents (67.67%) received medium scores, while about one-fifth (19.67%) received high scores. Only 12.67% received low scores. The categories of achievement motivation have been correlated with the independent variables and the analysis has been presented in the following pages.

GENDER AND ACHIEVEMENT MOTIVATION

According to the null hypothesis there will be no gender difference with regard to achievement motivation. In order to test this hypothesis these two variables were co-related and the analysis has been presented in Table 3.2.

Table 3.2: Distribution of Respondents According to their Gender and Level of Achievement Motivation

Gender Categories	Achievement Motivation Categories			
	Low	Medium	High	Total
Male	24 15.69%	102 66.67%	27 17.65%	153 51.00%
Female	14 9.52%	101 68.71%	32 21.77%	147 49.00%
Total	**38** **12.67%**	**203** **67.67%**	**59** **19.67%**	**300** **100%**

$\chi^2 = 2.941$; df = 2; P > 10.0

The analysis presented in the foregoing table indicates that there were no substantial differences in the achievement motivation levels of male and female students. However, the proportion of female students was a little higher in the high motivation category (21.77%) as compared to the male students in whose case the corresponding percentage was 17.65%. The chi-square test also indicates there is not a very significant association between these two variables. This finding is in conformity with the null-hypothesis in this context.

FIELD OF STUDY AND ACHIEVEMENT MOTIVATION

The null hypothesis in this regard states that there will be no differences in achievement motivation of the students from different fields of study. In order to test this hypothesis these two variables were co-related and the analysis has been presented in Table 3.3.

Table 3.3: Distribution of Respondents According to their Field of Study and Level of Achievement Motivation

Area of Study	Achievement Motivation Categories			
	Low	Medium	High	Total
Arts	14 9.33%	103 68.67%	33 22.00%	150 50.00%
Commerce	24 16.00%	100 66.67%	26 17.33%	150 50.00%
Total	**38** **12.67%**	**203** **66.67%**	**59** **19.67%**	**300** **100%**

$\chi^2 = 3.506$; df = 2; P > 5.0

The analysis presented in the foregoing table reveals that there is not much difference in the levels of achievement motivation among the students of 'Arts' and 'Commerce' streams. The chi-square test also indicates that there is no significant association between these two variables. However, the analysis indicates that the proportion of 'Arts' students was a little higher in the high achievement motivation category (22%) as compared to the students of 'Commerce' in whose case the corresponding percentage was 17.33%. This finding is in conformity with the null hypothesis in this regard.

AREA OF RESIDENCE AND ACHIEVEMENT MOTIVATION

The achievement motivation categories have been co-related with the area of residence of the respondents and the analysis of data has been presented in Table 3.4.

The analysis presented in the table indicates that a higher proportion (29.33%) of the respondents residing in the rural area had received high motivation scores as compared to those residing in the urban areas (10%). This finding indicates that the students belonging to rural areas have a stronger desire for achievement as they want to compete with the urban students. Moreover, when the rural students come to the college level they have to work harder as compared to the urban students. The analysis shows that very few rural students. (10%) had received low motivation scores. The chi-square test also depicts a highly significant association between these two variables.

Table 3.4: Distribution of Respondents According to their Area of Residence and Level of Achievement Motivation

Area of Residence	Achievement Motivation Categories			
	Low	Medium	High	Total
Rural	15 10.00%	91 60.67%	44 29.33%	150 50%
Urban	23 15.33%	112 74.67%	15. 10.00%	150 50%
Total	**38** **12.67%**	**203** **67.67%**	**59** **19.67%**	**300** **100%**

$\chi^2 = 18.111$; df = 2; $p > 0.1$

OCCUPATION OF PARENTS/GUARDIANS AND ACHIEVEMENT MOTIVATION

Occupation is one of the major social determinants of an individual's economic status. It does not determine only his lifestyle, rather if affects the ways of living of all the family members. Thus occupation of an individual can affect the ways of life of all members of the family. An attempt has been made to find out the impact of parent's/guardian's occupations on the motivation level of the students. The analysis in this context has been presented in the Table 3.5

The analysis presented in the table reveals that a higher proportion of the respondents (27.56%) whose parents/ guardians were engaged in low status jobs had received high motivation scores as compared to those whose parents/

guardians were in high status jobs (9.76%). This finding indicates that the students from the lower strata have a stronger desire to work hard and achieve something in life as compared to the students belonging to the upper strata. The chi-square test also indicates a significant association between these two variables.

Table 3.5: Distribution of Respondents According to the Occupation of their Parent/Guardian and Levels of Achievement Motivation

Occupation Parent/Guardian	Achievement Motivation Categories			
	Low	Medium	High	Total
Jobs (High Status)	11 26.83%	26 63.41%	4 9.76%	41 13.67%
Jobs (Low status)	17 13.39%	75 59.06%	35 27.56%	127 42.33
Business	6 5.94%	78 77.23%	17 16.83%	101 33.67%
Agriculture	4 12.90%	24 77.42%	3 9.68%	31 10.33%
Total	**38** **12.67%**	**203** **67.67%**	**59** **19.67%**	**300** **100%**

$\chi^2 = 3.867$; df = 2; P> 5.0

INCOME OF PARENTS/GUARDIANS AND ACHIEVEMENT MOTIVATION

In order to find out the economic status of an individual it is essential to know his/her income. In present day society the economic and social status are closely linked with one another. The socio-economic status of an individual exercises a significant influence on his psychology and social behaviour. However, the respondents of the present study were students and therefore did not have an income of their own. They were therefore asked to indicate the income of their parents/ guardians. This variable was cross-tabulated with the level of their achievement motivation and the analysis has been presented in Table 3.6.

Table 3.6: Distribution of Respondents According to their Parents/Guardians Income and Level of Achievement Motivation

Parents/Guardians Income	Achievement Motivation Categories			
	Low	**Medium**	**High**	**Total**
Upto 5 thousand	14 12.96%	69 63.89%	25 23.15%	108 36.00
5-10 thousand	12 9.16%	92 70.23%	27 20.61	131 43.67
Above10 thousand	12 19.67%	42 68.85%	7 11.48%	61 20.33%
Total	**38** **12.67%**	**203** **67.67%**	**59** **19.67%**	**300** **100%**

$\chi^2 = 6.816$; df = 4; P > 2.5

The analysis shown in the above table indicates that the level of achievement motivation of the respondents increases with a decrease in the income of their parents/guardians. In case of high income category only 11.48% of the respondents received high motivational scores whereas the corresponding percentage in the low income category was 23.15%. This analysis indicates that the students belonging to lower economic status families had a desire to achieve excellence in life whereas those students who belonged to high income families did not have the required motivation for achievement. The chi-square test also reveals a significant association between these two variables.

EDUCATIONAL LEVEL OF THE FAMILY AND ACHIEVEMENT MOTIVATION

It is generally believed that the educational level of a family significantly affects the life patterns of an individual. Accordingly it was considered essential to find out whether the educational level of the family has any bearing on the achievement level of its members or not. The procedure for the classification of families in different educational levels has already been explained in chapter III. The cross-tabulation between these two variables has been presented in Table 3.7.

Table 3.7: Distribution of Respondents According to Educational Levels of their Families and the Levels of Achievement Motivation

Educational Level Categories	Achievement Motivation Categories			
	Low	Medium	High	Total
Upto 4	4 18.18%	17 77.27%	1 4.55%	22 7.33%
5-8	18 11.92%	100 66.23%	33 21.85%	151 50.33%
Above 8	16 12.60%	86 67.72%	25 19.69%	127 42.34%
Total	**38** **12.67%**	**203** **67.67%**	**59** **19.67%**	**300** **100%**

$\chi^2 = 3.867$; df = 4; P > 5.0

The analysis of data presented in the above table reveals that a significantly higher proportion of respondents whose families had received medium and high education scores were placed in high achievement motivation category (21.85% and 19.69%). On the other hand, only one respondent whose family had received low education score was placed in the high motivation category (4.55%). Thus the analysis indicates that the students belonging to the better educated families depict a trend towards achievement of excellence as compared to the students from less educated families. The chi-square test also indicates a significant association between these two variables.

CASTE AFFILIATION AND ACIIIEVEMENT MOTIVATION

In the Indian society the significance of caste in social life cannot be ignored. Although as a result of the process of modernization some features of the traditional caste system have been weakened yet this institution has gained strength in some other aspects. The caste system still holds an important place in the social set-up of India. Accordingly, it was considered of interest to find out whether the caste affiliation of an individual has any bearing on the level of his achievement motivation or not. The variables of caste and levels of achievement motivation were cross-tabulated and the analysis has been presented in Table 3.8.

Table 3.8: Distribution of Respondents According to their Caste Affiliations and Levels of Achievement Motivation

Caste Categories	Achievement Motivation Categories			
	Low	Medium	High	Total
High	10 16.67%	37 61.67%	13 (21.67)%	60
Medium	19 13.10%	112 71.34%	26 16.56%	157
Low	8 10.26%	54 69.23%	16 20.51%	78
Total	**37**	**37**	**55**	**295**

* The five Muslim families have been excluded from the analysis.

The analysis of data presented in the foregoing table depicts that there are no substantial differences in the levels of achievement motivation of the respondents belonging to various caste categories. This finding is in conformity with the null hypothesis.

RELIGIOUS GROUPS AND ACHIEVEMENT MOTIVATION

Religion is another institution of great significance in the Indian society. The beliefs, attitudes and social behaviour of an individual are greatly influenced by the religion he practices. Therefore, it was considered of interest to find out whether the religion of an individual has any relationship with the level of his achievement motivation or not. In order to explore this relationship the two variables were cross-tabulated and the analysis of data have been presented in Table 3.9.

Table 3.9: Distribution of Respondents According to Religious Groups and Levels of Achievement Motivation

Religious group categories	Achievement Motivation Categories			
	Low	Medium	High	Total
Sikh	7 6.60%	77 72.64%	22 20.75%	106 35.33%
Hindu	28 14.81%	124 65.61%	37 19.58%	189 63.00%
Muslim	3 60.00%	2 40.00%	—	15 1.67%
Total	**38** **12.67%**	**203** **67.67%**	**59** **19.67%**	**300** **100%**

$\chi^2 = 14.72$; df = 4; $P > 0.1$

The analysis of data presented in the previous table indicates that there were no significant differences in the levels of achievement motivation of the respondents belonging to different religious groups. However, none of the Muslim students was placed in the high achievement motivation category. On the other hand, almost a similar proportion of students from Hindu and Sikh religious categories were placed in the high achievement motivation category.

TYPE OF FAMILY AND ACHIEVEMENT MOTIVATION

The type of family in which an individual resides has a significant bearing on his social behaviour as well as the psychological aspect. Therefore, it was considered of interest to find out whether the type of family in which an individual lives has any bearing on the level of his achievement motivation or not. These two variables were co-related and the analysis of data has been presented in Table 3.10.

Table 3.10: Distribution of Respondents According to type of Family and Levels of Achievement Motivation

Family Type Categories	Achievement Motivation Categories			
	Low	Medium	High	Total
Nuclear	18 9.63%	127 67.91%	42 22.46%	187 62.33%
Joint	13 14.44%	62 68.89%	15 16.67%	90 30.00%
Quasi-Joint	7 30.43%	14 60.87%	2 8.70%	23 7.67%
Total	**38** **12.67%**	**203** **67.67%**	**59** **19.67%**	**300** **100%**

$\chi^2 = 10.062$; df = 2; P > 0.5

The analysis of data presented in the preceding table indicates that there were no significant differences in the levels of achievement motivation of the respondents residing in different types of families. However, the proportion of students living in the nuclear families is little higher in the high achievement motivation category (22.46%) as compared to those living in joint or quasi-joint families in whose case the corresponding percentages are (16.67%) and (8.70%) respectively. The chi- square test indicates that the two variables are associated at 5% level of significance. The chi-square test reveals a significant association between these two variables.

The respondents were also asked a few question which were thought to be affecting their achievement motivation. First of all they were asked whether they like their teachers or not. Their responses have been presented in Table 3.11.

The data presented in the table below shows that about three-fourth of the respondents mentioned that they liked their teachers, 15.33% were undecided and only 8.67% mentioned that they did not like their teachers.

Table 3.11: Distribution of Respondents According to their liking for Teachers

Liking for teaches	Frequency	Percentage
Yes	228	76.00%
No	26	8.67%
Undecided	46	15.33%
Total	**300**	**100.00%**

The liking for teachers was co-related with the independent variables and some of the significant associations between the dependent and independent variables have been presented as under.

The area of residence of the respondents was cross-tabulated with the liking for teachers and the analysis has been presented in Table 3.12.

Table 3.12: Distribution of Respondents According to Area of Residence and Liking for Teachers

Area of Residence	Liking for teachers			
	Yes	No	Undecided	Total
Rural	124 82.67%	11 7.33%	15 10.00%	150 50%
Urban	104 69.33%	15 10.00%	31 20.67%	150 50%
Total	**228 76.00%**	**26 8.67%**	**46 15.33%**	**300 100%**

$\chi^2 = 7.93$; df = 2; P > 2.5

The analysis presented in the table above indicates that a higher proportion of the respondents residing in the rural area mentioned that they liked their teachers (82.67%) as compared to the urban residents in whose case the corresponding percentage was 69.33%. The chi- square test also corroborates a significant association between these two variables.

The liking for teachers was also cross-tabulated with the field of study and the analysis has been presented in Table 3.13.

Table 3.13: Distribution of Respondents According to their Field of Study and Liking for Teachers

Field of Study	Liking for teachers			
	Yes	No	Undecided	Total
Arts	124 82.67%	12 8.00%	14 9.33%	150 50%
Commerce	104 69.33%	14 9.33%	32 21.35%	150 50%
Total	**228** **76.00%**	**26** **8.67%**	**46** **15.33%**	**300** **100%**

$\chi^2 = 8.952$; df = 2; P > 2.5

The analysis in Table 3.13 reveals that a higher proportion of 'Arts' students mentioned that they liked their teachers (82.67%) as compared to the 'Commerce' students in whose case the corresponding percentage was 69.33%. The chi- square test also depicts a significant association between the two variables.

The liking for teachers was also cross-tabulated with the occupation of parents/guardians of the respondents and the analysis has been presented in the Table 3.14.

The analysis of data presented in the table indicates that a higher proportion of respondents whose parents/guardians were engaged in lower status jobs mentioned that they liked their teachers (82.68%) as compared to respondents whose parents/guardians were engaged in high status jobs (58.54%). The chi-square test also reveals a significant association between the two variables.

The respondents were further asked whether in their opinion only educated persons get respect in the society. There responses are shown in Table 3.15.

Table 3.14: Distribution of Respondents According to the Occupation of their Parents/Guardian and Liking for Teachers

Occupation of Parents/Guardians	Liking for Teachers			
	Yes	No	Undecided	Total
Jobs (High status)	24 58.54%	3 7.32%	14 34.15%	41(100) 13.67%
Jobs (Low status)	105 82.68%	10 7.87%	12 9.45%	127(100) 42.33%
Business	77 76.24%	8 7.92%	16 15.84%	101(100) 33.67%
Agriculture	22 70.97%	5 16.13%	4 12.90%	31(100) 10.33%
Total	**228 76.00%**	**26 8.67%**	**46 15.33%**	**300 100%**

$\chi^2 = 17.19$; df = 6; P > 1.0

Table 3.15: Distribution of Respondents According to their Perception about Importance of Education

Importance of Education	Frequency	Percentage
Perceive importance of education	135	45.00%
Do not perceive importance of education	116	38.67%
Undecided	49	16.33%
Total	**300**	**100.00%**

The data presented in Table 3.15 indicates that less than half of the respondents (45%) perceived the importance of education. A substantial number of respondents (16.33%) were undecided in this regard while more than one third (38.67%) did not perceive any importance of education.

The perception about the importance of education was cross-tabulated with the place of residence and the analysis has been presented in Table 3.16.

Table 3.16: Distribution of Respondents According to their Place of Residence and the Perception about Importance of Education

Place of Residence	Perception about Importance of Education			
	Perceive Importance	Do not Perceive Importance	Undecided	Total
Rural	60 40.00%	54 36.00%	36 24.00%	150 50%
Urban	75 50.00%	62 41.33%	13 8.67%	150 50%
Total	**135** **45.00%**	**116** **38.67%**	**49** **16.33%**	**300** **100%**

$\chi^2 = 13.01$; df = 2; P > 0.5

The analysis presented in the above table indicates that a substantially higher proportion of the rural respondents (24%) were not clear about the importance of education as they were undecided in this context. On the other hand very few (8.67%) of the urban respondents were undecided about the importance of education. Moreover a higher proportion of urban respondents (50%) perceived the importance of education as compared to the rural respondents (40%). The chi- square test also reveals a significant association between the two variables.

The field of study of the respondents was cross tabulated with the perception about the importance of education and the analysis has been presented in the Table 3.17.

The analysis of data shown in the table below indicates that a substantially higher proportion of 'Arts' students (53.33%) perceived the importance of education as compared to the 'Commerce' students (36.76%). The chi-square test also refers to a significant association between the two variables.

Table 3.17: Distribution of Respondents According to the Field of Study and Perception about Importance of Education

Field of Study	Perception about Importance of Education			
	Perceive Importance	Do not Perceive Importance	Undecided	Total
Arts	80 53.33%	47 31.33%	23 15.33%	150 50.00%
Commerce	55 36.76%	69 46.00%	26 17.33%	150 50.00%
Total	**135** **45.00%**	**116** **38.67%**	**49** **16.33%**	**300** **100%**

$\chi^2 = 8.98$; df = 2; P > 2.5

An effort was also made to know the liking of the students about their studies. They were asked to mention whether they will be pleased to miss the classes for some days or not. Their responses are presented in Table 3.18.

Table 3.18: Distribution of Respondents According to their liking of Studies

Liking of Studies	Frequency	Percentage
Like studies	104	34.67%
Do not like	196	65.33%
Total	**300**	**100.00%**

The data presented in the table indicates that a majority of the respondents (65.33%) did not like their studies as they mentioned that they would be pleased to miss their classes.

The liking of the studies was further cross-tabulated with the independent variables. Some of the significant associations between independent and the dependent variables have been described below.

The liking about studies was co-related with the gender of the respondents and the analysis has been presented in Table 3.19.

Table 3.19: Distribution of Respondents According to their Gender and Liking about Studies

Gender	Liking about Studies		
	Like Studies	Do not Like Studies	Total
Male	45 29.41%	108 70.59%	153 (51%)
Female	59 40.13%	88 59.87%	147 (49%)
Total	**104** **34.67%**	**196** **65.33%**	**300** **100%**

$\chi^2 = 4.82$; df = 1; P > 5.0.

The analysis of data presented in the table indicates that a higher proportion of the female respondents (40.13%) liked their studies as compared to the male respondents (29.41%). The chi-square test also demonstrates a significant association (at 5% level) between the two variables.

Further, the place of residence of the respondents was cross-tabulated with the liking for studies and the analysis has been presented in the Table 3.20.

The analysis of data presented in the table amply demonstrates that the rural students had more liking for their studies as compared to the urban students. The data reveals that a substantially higher proportion of the rural respondents (45.33%) liked their studies whereas the corresponding percentage for the urban students was 24%. The chi-square test also reveals a significant association (at 0.1% level) between these two variables.

Table 3.20: Distribution of Respondents According to their Place of Residence and Liking about Studies

Place of Residence	Liking about Studies		
	Like Studies	Do not Like Studies	Total
Rural	68 45.33%	82 (54.67%)	150 50%
Urban	36 24.00%	114 76.00%	150 50%
Total	**104** **34.67%**	**196** **65.33%**	**300** **100%**

$\chi^2 = 15.06$; df = 1; $P > 0.1$

The liking for studies was further co-related with the field of study and the analysis of data has been presented in Table 3.21.

Table 3.21: Distribution of Respondents According to their Field of Study and Liking about Studies

Field of Study	Liking about Studies		
	Like Studies	Do not Like Studies	Total
Arts	66 44.00%	84 56.00%	150 50%
Commerce	38 25.33%	112 74.67%	150 50%
Total	**104** **34.67%**	**196** **65.33%**	**300** **100%**

$\chi^2 = 11.52$; df = 1; $P > 0.1$

The analysis of data presented in the table clearly indicates that the 'Arts' students had more liking for their studies as compared to the 'Commerce' students. A substantially higher proportion of 'Arts' students (44%) did not want to miss their classes, whereas corresponding percentage for 'Commerce' students was 25.33%. The chi-square test also reveals a significant association between the two variables.

The liking about studies was further co-related with the educational scores of the family and the analysis of data has been presented in Table 3.22.

Table 3.22: Distribution of Respondents According to the Educational scores of their Families and Liking about Studies

Educational Scores of the family	Liking about Studies		
	Like Studies	Do not Like Studies	Total
Low	6 27.27%	16 72.73%	22
Medium	51 33.77%	100 66.23%	151
High	47 37.00%	80 63.00%	127
Total	**104** **34.67%**	**196** **65.33%**	**300** **100%**

$\chi^2 = 0.86$; df = 2; N.S.

The analysis of data presented in the table depicts that a lesser proportion of the respondents whose families had received low scores of education liked their studies (27.27%) as compared to those whose families had received medium educational scores (34.77%) and whose families had received high educational scores (37.00%). However, the chi-square test does not indicate any significant association between the two variables.

The liking about studies was also-co-related with the income of parents/guardians of the respondents and the analysis of data has been presented in Table 3.23.

Table 3.23: Distribution of Respondents According to the Income of Parents/Guardians and Liking about Studies

Income Categories	Liking about Studies		
	Like Studies	Do not Like Studies	Total
Low	62 57.40%	46 42.60%	108
Medium and High	42 21.87%	150 78.13%	192
Total	**104**	**196**	**300**

$\chi^2 = 38.4$; df = 1; P > 0.1.

The analysis of data presented in the table clearly indicates that a significantly higher proportion of the respondents whose parents/guardians income was less, liked their studies (57.40%) as compared to those whose parents/guardians had medium or high incomes (21.87%). The chi-square test also depicts a highly significant association between the two variables.

In order to find out the desire for learning among the students they were asked whether they enjoyed reading to learn more or not. Their responses have been shown in Table 3.24.

Table 3.24: Distribution of Respondents According to their Desire for Learning

Desire for Learning	Frequency	Percentage
Yes	127	42.33%
No	173	57.67%
Total	**300**	**100.00%**

The data presented in the table reveals that a majority of the respondents did not have a desire to learn more (57.67%).

The desire to learn was further co-related with other independent variables and some of the significant associations between the independent and the dependent variables have been shown in the ensuing analysis.

The desire to learn has been co-related with the gender of the respondents and the analysis has been shown in Table 3.25..

Table 3.25: Distribution of Respondents According to their Gender and Desire to Learn

Gender Categories	Desire to Learn		
	Yes	No	Total
Male	54 35.29%	99 64.71%	153
Female	73 49.66%	74 50.34%	147
Total	**127**	**173**	**300**

$\chi^2 = 6.32$; df = 1; P > 0.1.

The analysis of data shown in the table indicates that almost half of the female respondents (49.66%) exhibited a desire to learn more as compared to about one- third of the male respondents (35.29%). The chi-square test also reveals a significant association between the two variables.

The desire to learn was further cross-tabulated with the place of residence of the respondents and the analysis in this regard has been presented in Table 3.26.

Table 3.26: Distribution of Respondents According to their Place of Residence and Desire to Learn

Place of Residence	Desire to Learn		
	Yes	No	Total
Rural	68 45.33%	82 54.67%	150
Urban	59 39.33%	91 60.67%	150
Total	**127**	**173**	**300**

$\chi^2 = 1.00$; df = 1; P > 5.0.

The analysis of data presented in the table indicates that a slightly higher proportion of the respondents from the rural areas (45.33%) exhibited a desire to learn more as compared to the urban respondents (39.33%). However, the chi-square test does not show any significant association between the two variables.

The desire to learn more was also co-related with the educational scores of respondents families. For the purpose of analysis the categories of lower and medium educational scores have been clubbed together. The analysis in this context has been presented in Table 3.27.

Table 3.27: Distribution of Respondents According to the Educational Scores of their Families and the Desire to Learn

Educational Scores	**Desire to Learn**		
	Yes	**No**	**Total**
Low and Medium	56 32.36	117 67.64	173
High	71 55.90	56 44.10	127
Total	**127**	**173**	**300**

$\chi^2 = 16.65$; df = 1; $P > 0.1$.

The analysis of data presented in table amply demonstrates that a substantially higher proportion of the respondents whose families had received high educational scores (55.90%) exhibited a desire to learn more, whereas the corresponding percentage for families which had received lower and medium educational scores was 32.36%. The chi-square test also reveals a highly significant association between the two variables.

The desire to learn was also cross-tabulated with the income categories of respondents families. For the purpose of analysis the families with medium and high incomes have been clubbed together. The analysis in this regard has been presented in Table 3.28.

Table 3.28: Distribution of Respondents According to the Income Categories of their Families and Desire to Learn

Income Categories	Desire to Learn		
	Yes	**No**	**Total**
Low	59 54.63%	49 45.37%	108
Medium and High	68 35.42%	124 64.58%	192
Total	**127**	**173**	**300**

$\chi^2 = 10.43$; df = 1; $P > 0.1$.

The analysis of data presented in the previous table reveals that a higher proportion of the respondents whose families had low income (54.63%) exhibited a desire to learn more whereas the corresponding percentage in case of families with medium and high incomes was 35.42%. The chi-square test also indicates a highly significant association between the two variables.

CHAPTER - IV

SOCIO-ECONOMIC CORRELATES OF ACADEMIC PERFORMANCE

The academic performance of the students is one of the most important aspects of modern education. As a result of advancement of science, culture and civilization the people of modern societies have realized the importance of education. Education is expected to promote all-round growth of an individual – physical, mental, moral, social and intellectual. Thus the major objective of education is to draw out the best in an individual's body, mind and spirit. In the process of educating the young members of the society, a lot of stress has been laid on the evaluation of the students and the measurement of their achievement in various courses of study. For this purpose special stress has been laid on the assessment of the students with the help of the examination system, which has become an integral part of the modern system of education.

The level of academic performance depends upon various factors. The educational psychologists and sociologists have tried to focus on these factors. These factors are broadly divided into two groups, that is, the individual factors and the environmental factors. The individual factors which are considered to be important in academic performance include intelligence, personality and level of motivation of an individual. The environmental factors include both home and school environment. A number of studies have shown close interrelationship between motivation and academic performance of an individual. According to Vidhu Mohan (1972), "perhaps motivation in its widest connotation contributes significant amount to academic success. In the area of induced motivation, those children who were given free comments (both praise and blame) about their performance on an objective test, achieved higher scores on subsequent tests". Lowell (1952) found that individual's high n-Ach shows a higher level of performance on both arithmetic and verbal scales. Atkinson and Litwin (1960) reported a positive co-relation between n-Ach and persistence and performance in examination.

The academic performance of an individual can be measured with reference to the marks scored by him/her in various courses of study in the examinations. These marks give an overall idea about the scholastic achievements which can also be taken as an indicator of the level of intelligence of an individual. In the present study, percentage of total marks obtained by students in the previous final examinations conducted by the university were taken as an index of academic performance. The students who scored 60% or more marks in a subject were given a score of 3; those scoring between 50 to 60% marks were given a score of 2 and those scoring less than 50% marks were given a score of one. The scores for all the subjects were added to arrive at the total score received by each respondent. Based on the range of the scores they were classified in three categories of academic performance, i.e. high, medium and low.

The validity of these marks is taken for granted because they are accepted as the only criterion for admission to the next class or other courses as well as for employment purposes. Based on the percentage of marks secured by the respondents they were assigned scores and on the basis of the range of scores they were classified into three categories of high, medium and low academic performance. The distribution of respondents in these three categories has been presented in Table 4.1.

Table 4.1: Distribution of Respondents in the Academic Performance Categories

Academic performance categories	Frequency	Percentage
High	80	26.67
Medium	92	30.67
Low	128	42.67
Total	**300**	**100.00**

The data presented in the table indicates that the highest proportion of the respondents were placed in the low academic performance category, followed by 30.67% in the medium category and 26.67% in the high academic performance category.

The levels of academic performance were co-related with other socio-economic variables and the significant associations between the dependent and the independent variables have been presented in the ensuing pages.

AGE OF ACADEMIC PERFORMANCE

The levels of academic performance were cross-tabulated with the age categories of the respondents and the analysis of data in this context has been presented in the Table 4.2.

The analysis of data presented in Table 4.2 indicates that a substantially higher proportion of the respondents who were upto 18 years of age were placed in the high academic performance category (35.04%) whereas the corresponding percentage for the respondents above 18 years of age was 21.31%. The chi-square test also reveals a significant association between the two variables.

Table 4.2: Distribution of Respondents according to their Age Categories and Levels of Academic Performance

Age Categories	Levels of Academic Performance			
	High	Medium	Low	Total
Upto 18 years	41 (35.04)	36 (30.77)	40 (34.19)	117 (39.00)
Above 18 years	39 (21.31)	56 (30.60)	88 (48.09)	183 (61.00)
Total	**80 (26.67)**	**92 (30.67)**	**128 (42.67)**	**300 (100.00)**

$\chi^2 = 8.279$; df = 2; P > 1.0

GENDER AND ACADEMIC PERFORMANCE

The levels of academic performance were further co-related with the gender of the respondents. For the purpose of analysis the categories of high and medium academic performance were clubbed together. The analysis of data in this regard has been presented in Table 4.3.

Table 4.3: Distribution of Respondents according to their Gender and Levels of Academic Performance

Gender Categories	Levels of Academic Performance		
	High and Medium	Low	Total
Male	69 (45.10)	84 (54.90)	153
Female	103 (70.06)	44 (29.94)	147
Total	**172 (57.33)**	**128 (42.67)**	**300**

$\chi^2 = 19.08$; df = 1; P > 0.1

The analysis of data presented in the above table clearly indicates that a significantly higher proportion of the female respondents were placed in the high and medium academic performance categories (70.66%) as compared to the male respondents in whose case the corresponding percentage was 45.10%. The chi-square test demonstrates that there is a highly significant association between the two variables.

PLACE OF RESIDENCE AND ACADEMIC PERFORMANCE

The levels of academic performance were cross-tabulated with the place of residence of the respondents. For the purpose of analysis the categories of high and medium academic performance have been clubbed together. The analysis of data in this context have been presented in Table 4.4.

Table 4.4: Distribution of Respondents according to their Place of Residence and Levels of Academic Performance

Place of residence	**Levels of Academic Performance**		
	High and Medium	**Low**	**Total**
Rural	74 49.33%	76 50.67%	150 50%
Urban	98 65.33%	52 34.67%	150 50%
Total	**172** **57.33%**	**128** **42.67%**	**300** **100%**

$\chi^2 = 7.84$; df = 1; P > 0.5

The analysis of data presented in the table indicates that a higher proportion of the urban respondents had received medium and high academic performance scores (65.33%) whereas the corresponding percentage for the rural respondents was 49.33%. The chi-square test reveals that the two variables are significantly associated with the each other.

FIELD OF STUDY AND ACADEMIC PERFORMANCE

The levels of academic performance were further co-related with the field of the study of the respondents. For the purpose of analysis the categories of high and medium scores of academic performance have been clubbed together. The analysis of data in this regard have been presented in Table 4.5.

Table 4.5: Distribution of Respondents according to their Field of Study and Levels of Academic Performance

Field of Study	Levels of Academic Performance		
	High and Medium	Low	Total
Arts	107 71.33%	43 28.67%	150 50%
Commerce	65 43.33%	85 56.67%	150 50%
Total	**172** **57.33%**	**128** **42.67%**	**300** **100%**

$\chi^2 = 24.02$; df = 1; $P > 0.1$

The analysis of data presented in the table clearly indicates that a substantially higher proportion of 'Arts' students had received high and medium academic performance scores (71.33%) whereas the corresponding percentage for 'Commerce' students was 43.33%. The Chi-square test also depicts a highly significant association between the two variables.

EDUCATIONAL SCORES OF THE FAMILY AND ACADEMIC PERFORMANCE

The levels of academic performance were also cross-tabulated with the educational scores of the respondents' families. For the purpose of analysis low and medium educational score categories and high and medium academic performance score categories have been clubbed together. The analysis in this context has been presented in the Table 4.6.

The analysis of data presented in the below table indicates that a higher proportion of the respondents whose families had received high educational scores were placed in the high and medium academic performance categories (63.77%) as compared to the respondents whose families had received low and medium educational scores (52.62%). The Chi square test shows a significant association between the two variables at 5% level.

Table 4.6: Distribution of Respondents according to the Educational Scores of their Families and their Levels of Academic Performance

Educational Score Categories	Levels of Academic Performance		
	High and medium	Low	Total
Low and Medium	91 52.60%	82 47.40%	173
High	81 63.77%	46 36.23%	127
Total	**172** **57.33%**	**128** **42.67%**	**300** **100%**

$\chi^2 = 3.74$; df =1; P > 5.0

INCOME CATEGORIES AND ACADEMIC PERFORMANCE

The levels of academic performance were cross-tabulated with thc income categories of parents/guardians of the respondents. For the purpose of analysis the medium and high income categories as well as medium and high academic performance categories have been clubbed together. The analysis of data in this context has been presented in the Table 4.7.

The analysis of data presented in the below table demonstrates that a slightly higher proportion of the respondents whose parents/guardians had low incomes were placed In reply to: medium and high categories of academic performance (63.88%) while the corresponding percentage for medium and high income categories was 53.64%. The chi-square test also demonstrates a significant association between the two variables.

Table 4.7: **Distribution of Respondents according to Income Categories of Parents/Guardian's of the Respondents and the Levels of Academic Performance**

Income Categories	Levels of Academic Performance		
	High + Medium	Low	Total
High + medium	69 63.88%	39 36.12%	108
Low	103 54.64%	89 46.36%	192
Total	**172** **57.33%**	**128** **42.67%**	**300** **100%**

$\chi^2 = 2.94$; df = 1; P > 5.0

CASTE AND ACADEMIC PERFORMANCE

The levels of academic performance were also co-related with the caste categories of the respondents. The analysis of data in this context has been presented in Table 4.8.

Table 4.8: **Distribution of Respondents according to the Levels of Academic Performance and their Caste Categories**

Caste Categories	Levels of Academic Performance		
	High and Medium	Low	Total
High	29 48.33%	31 51.67%	60
Medium	92 58.60%	65 41.40%	157
Low	46 58.97%	32 41.03%	78
Total	**167**	**128**	**295**

$\chi^2 = 2.07$; df = 1; P > 10.0

The analysis of data presented in the table indicates that there were no significant differences in the levels of academic performance of the respondents belonging to various caste categories. However, a little higher proportion of medium and low caste respondents were placed in medium and high levels of academic performance as compared to the respondents belonging to the high caste category. The chi-square test does not reveal a significant association between these two variables.

SERIOUSNESS ABOUT STUDIES

An important dimension related to academic performance is the seriousness about studies. In order to find out the extent of seriousness about studies among the respondents of the present study they were asked to respond to ten statements in this context. Their responses were assigned scores and according to the range of the scores, the respondents were classified in three categories of low, medium and high seriousness about studies. The distribution of respondents according to these categories has been presented in Table 4.9.

Table 4.9: Distribution of Respondents according to Levels of Seriousness about Studies

Categories	Frequency	Percentage
Low	41	13.67
Medium	120	40.00
High	139	46.33
Total	**300**	**100.00**

The table shows that a higher proportion of the respondents (46.33%) were placed in the high category, followed by 40% in medium category of seriousness about studies. Only 13.67% of the respondents had a low level of seriousness about studies.

GENDER AND SERIOUSNESS ABOUT STUDIES

The levels of seriousness about studies were further correlated with other independent variables. Some of the significant associations have been presented in the following pages. For the purpose of analysis the categories of low and medium levels of seriousness about studies have been clubbed together.

The levels of seriousness about studies were correlated with the gender of the respondents and analysis of data in this context has been presented in Table 4.10.

Table 4.10: Distribution of Respondents according to Levels of Seriousness about Studies and their Gender

Gender Categories	Levels of Seriousness about Studies		
	Low and Medium	High	Total
Male	102 66.67%	51 33.33%	153
Female	59 40.14%	88 59.86%	147
Total	**161**	**139**	**300**

$\chi^2 = 5.24$; df = 1; $p > 1.0$

The analysis presented in the foregoing table reveals that a considerably higher proportion of the female respondents (59.86%) were placed in high seriousness category whereas, the corresponding percentage for the male respondents was 33.33%. The chi-square test also reveals a significant association between these two variables.

PLACE OF RESIDENCE AND SERIOUSNESS ABOUT STUDIES

The seriousness about studies were further cross-tabulated with the place of residence of the respondents and the analysis has been presented in the Table 4.11.

The table shows that a higher proportion of the rural respondents (54%) were placed in the high level of seriousness about studies whereas the corresponding percentage for the urban respondents was 38.67%. The chi-square test also indicates a significant association between these two variables.

Table 4.11: Distribution of Respondents according to Levels of Seriousness about Studies and their Place of Residence

Place of Residence	Levels of Seriousness about Studies		
	Low and Medium	High	Total
Rural	69 46%	81 54%	150
Urban	92 61.33%	58 38.67%	150
Total	**161**	**139**	**300**

$\chi^2 = 7.08$; df = 1; P > 1.0

EDUCATIONAL LEVELS OF FAMILY AND SERIOUSNESS ABOUT STUDIES

The levels of seriousness abut studies were also correlated with the educational scores of the respondents families and the analysis has been presented in Table 4.12.

Table 4.12: Distribution of Respondents according to Levels of Seriousness about Studies and Educational Levels of their Families

Educational Score Categories	Levels of seriousness about studies		
	Low and Medium	High	Total
Low and Medium	116 (67.05)	57 (32.95)	173
High	45 (35.43)	82 (64.57)	127
Total	**161**	**139**	**300**

$\chi^2 = 7.12$; df = 1; P > 1.0

The analysis of data presented in the foregoing table clearly indicates that a significantly higher proportion of the respondents whose families had received high educational scores were placed in the category of high level of seriousness about studies (64.57%) as compared to the respondents whose families had received low and medium educational scores (32.95%). The chi-square test also depicts a significant association between these two variables.

INCOME CATEGORIES AND SERIOUSNESS ABOUT STUDIES

The levels of seriousness about studies were further correlated with the income categories of their parents/ guardians and the analysis in this regard has been presented in Table 4.13.

Table 4.13: Distribution of Respondents according to Levels of Seriousness about Studies and Income Categories of Parents/Guardians of the Respondents

Income Categories	Levels of Seriousness about Studies		
	Low and Medium	High	Total
Low and medium	49 45.77%	59 54.63%	108
High	112 58.33%	80 41.67%	192
Total	**161**	**139**	**300**

$\chi^2 = 4.65$; df = 1; P > 5.0

The analysis of data presented in the table indicates that a higher proportion of the respondents whose parents/ guardians were placed in the low income category depicted higher level of seriousness about studies (54.63%) whereas the corresponding percentage for medium and high income categories was 41.67%. The chi-square test also indicates a significant association between these two variables at 5% level of significance.

REASONS FOR LOW ACADEMIC PERFORMANCE

An attempt has also been made to find out the reasons for low academic performance of students. The respondents who had received low academic performance scores were asked to respond to certain statements related to their college, their house, mental reasons, social reasons and economic reasons. Based on their responses they were assigned scores and depending upon the range of scores they were divided into two categories of low and high extent of the above mentioned factors.

ATTITUDE TOWARDS COLLEGE AND ACADEMIC PERFORMANCE

First of all the respondents with low academic achievement scores were asked to respond to certain statements related to their college. Those respondents who did not think that their college was responsible for their low academic achievement were given lower scores and those who thought their college to be responsible were given higher scores. The distribution of respondents according to their attitude towards their college indicated that 59.38% were placed in the low category while the remaining 40.62% were in the high category.

GENDER AND ATTITUDE TOWARDS COLLEGE

The attitude of the low achievers towards their college were correlated with the gender of the respondents and the analysis of data has been presented in Table 4.14.

Table 4.14: Distribution of Low Achievers according to their Gender and Attitude towards College

Gender	**Categories of Attitude towards College**		
	Low	**High**	**Total**
Male	43 51.19%	41 48.81%	84
Female	33 75.0%	11 25.0%	44
Total	**76**	**52**	**128**

$\chi^2 = 6.77$; df =1; P > 1.0

The analysis of data presented in the table indicates that a significantly higher proportion of female low achievers did not have a negative attitude towards their college (75%) whereas the corresponding percentage for the male low achievers was 51.19%. The chi-square test also indicates a significant association between these two variables.

PLACE OF RESIDENCE AND ATTITUDE TOWARDS COLLEGE

The attitude towards their college of the low achievers was also correlated with their place of residence and the analysis of data in this regard has been presented in Table 4.15.

Table 4.15: Distribution of Low Achievers according to their Place of Residence and Attitude towards College

Place of Residence	**Categories of Attitude towards College**		
	Low	**High**	**Total**
Rural	39 (51.32%)	37 (48.68%)	76
Urban	37 (71.15%)	15 (28.85%)	52
Total	**76**	**52**	**128**

$\chi^2 = 7.12$; df= 1; p> 0.5

The analysis of data in the preceding table clearly indicates that a higher proportion of low achievers residing the rural areas did not have a favourable attitude towards their college (48.68%) whereas the corresponding percentage for the urban low achievers was 28.85%. This might be due to the fact that there are lesser facilities in the rural colleges as compared to the urban colleges. The chi-square test also reveals a significant association between these two variables.

INCOME AND ATTITUDES TOWARDS COLLEGE

The analysis was carried further and the attitude towards college of the low achievers was co-related with the income categories of their parents/guardians. The analysis in this context has been presented in Table 4.16.

Table 4.16: Distribution of Low Achievers according to the Income Categories of their Parents/Guardians and Attitude towards College

Income categories	**Categories of Attitude towards College**		
	Low	**High**	**Total**
Medium and high	18 (46.15%)	21 (53.85%)	39
Low	58 (65.17%)	31 (34.83%)	89
Total	**76**	**52**	**128**

$\chi^2 = 4.04$; df=1; p>5.0

The analysis presented in the foregoing table indicates that a higher proportion of the respondents (53.85%) whose parents/guardians were placed in the medium and high income categories did not have favourable attitude towards their college as compared to the respondents from lower income families (34.83%). The chi-square test also reveals a significant association between the two variables.

HOUSING CONDITIONS AND LOW ACADEMIC PERFORMANCE

The respondents were also asked to respond to some statements, related to their house in order to find out whether their housing conditions were responsible for their low academic performance or not. The responses to various statements were assigned scores and depending on the range of scores the respondents were classified into two categories of low and high. The low category consists of those respondents who do not think that the housing problem is very serious and the high category includes those respondents who think that the housing problem is quite serious. The analysis of data revealed that about two-thirds of the low achievers (67.19%) were of the view that the housing problem was not very serious and thus they were included in the 'low' category. The remaining about one third of the low achievers (32.81%) perceived housing problem to be an important cause for their low academic performance.

The analysis was carried further and the perception of the low achievers about their house were co-related with the independent variables. Some of the significant associations between the concerned variables have been presented below.

GENDER AND HOUSING PROBLEM

The perceptions of the low achievers about the housing problem was co-related with the gender of the respondents. The analysis in this context has been presented in Table 4.17.

Table 4.17: Distribution of Low Achievers according to their Gender and Perception about Housing Problem

Gender	Perception about Housing Problem		
	Low	High	Total
Male	70 (83.33%)	14 (16.67%)	84
Female	16 (36.37%)	28 (63.63%)	44
Total	**86**	**42**	**128**

$\chi^2 = 28.88$; df=1; P> 0.1

The analysis of data presented in the table clearly indicates that a significantly higher proportion of the female low achievers perceived housing to be a serious problem (63.63%) whereas the corresponding percentage for the male low achieves was only 16.67%. The chi-square test also depicts a highly significant association between the two variables.

PLACE OF RESIDENCE AND HOUSING PROBLEMS

The perception regarding the housing problem of low achievers was co-related with their place of residence. The analysis in this regard has been presented in Table 4.18.

Table 4.18: Distribution of Low Achievers according to their Perception of Housing Problem and their Place of Residence

Place of Residence	Perception of housing problem		
	Low	**High**	**Total**
Rural	48 (63.16%)	28 (36.84%)	76
Urban	38 (73.08%)	14 (26.92%)	52
Total	**86**	**42**	**128**

$\chi^2 = 1.35$; df = 1; N.S.

The analysis of data presented in the table indicates that a higher proportion of the low achievers from the rural area perceived housing problem to be serious (36.84%) as compared to the low achieves from urban areas (26.92%). However, the chi-square test does not reveal any significant association between the two variables.

INCOME AND HOUSING PROBLEM

The perception of the low achievers about the housing problem was co-related with the income categories of their parents/guardians. The analysis with regard to these two variables has been presented in Table 4.19.

The analysis of data presented in the table indicates that a considerably higher proportion of the low achievers whose parents/guardians had low income perceived housing problems to be serious (39.33%) as compared to those from medium and high income families (17.95%). The chi-square test also depicts a significant association between the two variables.

Table 4.19: Distribution of Low Achievers according to their Perception of Housing Problem and Income Categories of their Parents/Guardians

Income Categories	Perception of Housing Problem		
	Low	**High**	**Total**
Medium and high	32 (82.05%)	7 (17.95%)	39
Low	54 (60.67%)	35 (39.33%)	89
Total	**86**	**42**	**128**

$\chi^2 = 5.60$; df =1; p> 2.5

HEALTH AND LOW ACADEMIC PERFORMANCE

Those respondents whose level of academic performance was lower were asked to respond to certain statements related to their health. Their responses were assigned scores and based on the range of scores they were divided into two categories of low and high. The low category included those low achievers who did not consider health to be serious cause for their low academic performance; while the high category included those respondents who considered health to be a serious cause for their low academic performance. The analysis of data indicated that about three-fourths (75.78%) of the low achievers did not consider health to be a major cause for their low academic performance. The remaining about one-fourths (24.22%) of the low achievers attributed their low academic performance to the health problems.

PLACE OF RESIDENCE AND HEALTH PROBLEMS

The views of the low achievers about their health problems were further co- related with the independent variables. Some of the significant associations between these two types of variables have been presented below.

The view of the respondents about their heath problems were co-related with their place of residence and the analysis has been presented in Table 4.20.

Table 4.20: Distribution of Low Achievers according to their Health Problems and their Place of Residence

Place of Residence	Health Problems		
	Low	High	Total
Rural	68 (89.47%)	8 (10.53%)	76
Urban	29 (55.77%)	23 (44.23%)	52
Total	**97**	**31**	**128**

$\chi^2 = 19.15$; df = 1; p > 0.1

The analysis of data presented in the table clearly indicates that a significantly higher proportion of the urban low achievers considered health to be a serious problem (44.23%) as compared to the rural low achievers in whose case the corresponding parentage was only 10.53%. The chi-square test also indicates a highly significant association between the two variables.

INCOME AND HEALTH PROBLEMS

The views of low achievers about their health problems were further co-related with the income categories of their parents/guardians and the analysis has been presented Table 4.21.

Table 4.21: Distribution of Low Achievers according to their Health Problems and their Parents/ Guardians Income Categories

Income Categories	Health Problems		
	Low	High	Total
Medium and high	33 (84.61%)	6 (15.39%)	39
Low	64 (71.91%)	25 (29.09%)	89
Total	**97**	**31**	**128**

$\chi^2 = 2.86$; df= 31; p> 10.0

The analysis of data in table indicates that a higher proportion of the low achievers from low income families perceived health as a major problem (29.09%) as compared to those belonging to medium and high income families in whose case the corresponding percentage was 15.39%. However, the chi-square test does not reveal a very significant association between the two variables.

PSYCHOLOGICAL REASONS FOR LOW ACADEMIC PERFORMANCE

In order to find out whether any psychological reasons were responsible for low academic performance, the respondents were asked to respond to a few statements related to their involvement in studies, depression, their mental level and their attitudes towards examinations. The responses of the respondents were assigned scores and according to the range of the scores they were divided into two categories of low and high. Those in the low category exhibited lesser psychological problems as compared to those in the high category. The distribution of respondents in these two categories revealed that a little higher proportion of the low achievers (56.25%) were placed in the high category and the remaining 43.75% in the low category.

The psychological factors related to low academic performance were further co related with the independent variables and some of the significant associations between these two types of variables have been presented below.

GENDER AND PSYCHOLOGICAL REASONS

The psychological factors were cross tabulated with the gender of the respondents and the analysis has been presented in the Table 4.22.

The analysis of data presented in the foregoing table indicates that a higher proportion of the female low achievers had lesser psychological problems (61.36%) whereas the corresponding percentage for the male low achievers was 34.52%. The chi-square test also shows a highly significant association between the two variables.

Table 4.22: Distribution of Low Achievers according to the Gender of the Respondents and the Psychological Reasons

Gender	Psychological Problems		
	Low	High	Total
Male	29 (34.52%)	55 (65.48%)	84
Female	27 (61.36%)	17 (38.64%)	44
Total	**56**	**72**	**128**

$\chi^2 = 8.44$; df=1; p> 0.5

PLACE OF RESIDENCE AND PSYCHOLOGICAL REASONS

The psychological problems of the low achievers were further co-related with their place of residence and the analysis in this context has been presented in Table 4.23.

Table 4.23: Distribution of Low Achievers according to their Place of Residence and the Psychological Problems

Place of Residence	Psychological Problems		
	Low	High	Total
Rural	25 (32.89)	51 (67.11)	76
Urban	31 (59.61)	21 (40.39)	52
Total	**56**	**72**	**128**

$\chi^2 = 8.96$; df=1; p> 0.5

The data given in the table depicts that a higher proportion of those low achievers who were residing in the urban areas (59.61%) reported lesser psychological problems as compared to the rural low achievers in whose case the corresponding percentage was 32.89%. The chi-square test also reveals a highly significant association between the two variables.

EDUCATIONAL SCORES OF THE FAMILY AND PSYCHOLOGICAL REASONS

The psychological problems of the low achievers were further co-related with the educational scores of their families and the analysis of data in this regard has been presented in Table 4.24.

Table 4.24: Distribution of Low Achievers according to the Educational Scores of their Families and the Psychological Problems

Educational score of the family	Psychological Problems		
	Low	High	Total
Low and Medium	29 (35.36%)	53 (64.64%)	82
High	27 (58.69%)	19 (41.31%)	46
Total	**56**	**72**	**128**

$\chi^2 = 6.49$; df=1; p>1.0

The analysis of data shown in the previous table depicts that a higher proportion of those low achievers whose families had received high educational scores reported lesser psychological problems (58.69%) as compared to those whose families had received low and medium educational scores, in whose case the corresponding percentage was 35.36%. The chi-square test also shows a significant association between the two variables.

INCOME AND PSYCHOLOGICAL REASONS

The psychological problems of the low achievers were also co-related with the income categories of their parents/ guardians. The analysis of data with regard to these two variables has been presented in Table 4.25.

Table 4.25: Distribution of Low Achieves according to the Income Category of their Parents/Guardians and the Psychological Problems

Income Category	Psychological Problems		
	Low	High	Total
High and medium	22 (56.41%)	17 (43.59%)	39
Low	34 (38.20%)	55 (61.80%)	89
Total	**56**	**72**	**128**

$\chi^2 = 3.85$; df=1; p> 5.0

The analysis of data shown in the table indicates that a higher proportion of the low achievers whose parents/guardians had lower income reported more psychological problems (61.80%) as compared to those whose families had medium and high incomes, in whose case the corresponding percentage was 43.59%. The chi-square test also depicts a significant association between the two variables.

SOCIAL REASONS FOR LOW ACADEMIC PERFORMANCE

The low achievers were asked to respond to some statements related to their social interaction. Based on their responses they were assigned scores and according to the range of the scores they were divided into two categories of low and high. Those who were placed in the low category had limited social interaction whereas, the sphere of social interaction was wider in case of those included in the high category. The analysis of data reveled that almost the same proportion of the low achievers were placed in both the categories. The percentage of low achievers in the low category was 47.65% and it was 52.35% in case of the high category.

The pattern of social interaction of the low achievers was co-related with the independent variables. Some of the significant associations between these two types of variables have been discussed in the following pages.

PLACE OF RESIDENCE AND SOCIAL REASONS

The pattern of social interaction of the low achievers was cross- tabulated with their place of residence and the analysis in this context has been presented in Table 4.26.

Table 4.26: Distribution of Low Achievers according to their Place of Residence and Pattern of Social Interaction

Place of Residence	Pattern of social interaction		
	Low	High	Total
Rural	42 (55.26%)	34 (44.74%)	76
Urban	19 (36.53%)	33 (63.47%)	52
Total	**61**	**67**	**128**

$\chi^2 = 3.84$; df= 1; $p > 5.0$

The analysis of data presented in the table indicates that a higher proportion of the respondents residing in the urban areas had wider sphere of social interaction (63.47%) whereas the corresponding percentage for those residing in the rural areas was 44.74%. The chi-square test also indicates a significant association between the two variables.

INCOME AND SOCIAL REASONS

The pattern of social interaction of the low achievers was co-related with the income categories of their parents/ guardians. The analysis in this context has been presented in Table 4.27.

The analysis of data shown in the table below indicates that a higher proportion of the low achievers whose parents/ guardians were placed in the medium and high income category had a wider sphere of social interaction (61.54%) whereas the corresponding percentage for those who were in the lower income category was 48.31%. However, the chi-square test does not reveal any significant association between the two variables.

Table 4.27: Distribution of Low Achievers according to the Income Categories of their Parents/Guardians and Pattern of Social Interaction

Income Categories	Pattern of social Interaction		
	Low	High	Total
High and medium	15 (38.46%)	24 (61.54%)	39
Low	46 (51.69%)	43 (48.31%)	89
Total	**61**	**67**	**128**

$\chi^2 = 1.88$; df=1; N.S

CASTE AND SOCIAL REASONS

The sphere of social interaction of the low achievers was also co-related with their caste background. The analysis of data in this context has been shown in Table 4.28.

Table 4.28: Distribution of Low Achievers according to their Caste Background and Pattern of Social Interaction

Caste Background	Pattern of social interaction		
	Low	High	Total
High and Medium	40 (41.67%)	56 (58.33%)	96
Low	21 (65.63%)	11 (34.37%)	32
Total	**61**	**67**	**128**

$\chi^2 = 6.03$; df=1; $P > 2.5$

The analysis of data presented in the above table reveals that a higher proportion of the low achievers belonging to high and medium castes had a wider sphere of social interaction (58.33%) whereas the corresponding percentage for the low caste group was 34.37%. The chi-square test also demonstrates that there is a significant association between the two variables at 2.5 level of significance.

ECONOMIC REASONS AND LOW ACADEMIC PERFORMANCE

The low achievers were further asked to respond to a few statements regarding their economic conditions in order to find out whether the economic reasons were responsible for their low academic performance. Their response were assigned scores and on the basis of the range of the scores they were divided into two categories of low and high. Those included in the low category did not think economic reasons to be very important, while those in the high category considered economic reasons as very important for their low academic performance. The analysis of data revealed that a majority of the low achievers 57.03% considered economic reasons as very important while 42.97% did not think them to be so important for their low academic performance.

The economic reasons for low academic performance were cross-tabulated with the independent variables and some of the important associations between the two type of variables have been presented in the following pages.

PLACE OF RESIDENCE AND ECONOMIC REASONS

The economic reasons mentioned by low achievers were cross- tabulated with their place of residence and the analysis in this context has been presented in Table 4.29.

Table 4.29: Distribution of Low Achievers according to their Place of Residence and the Economic Reasons

Place of Residence	Economics reasons		
	Low	High	Total
Rural	27 (35.52%)	49 (64.48%)	76
Urban	28 (53.84%)	24 (46.16%)	52
Total	**55**	**73**	**128**

$\chi^2 = 3.90$; df= 1; p> 5.0

The analysis of data presented in the table depicts that a higher proportion of the low achievers residing in the rural areas considered economic reasons as very important for their low academic performance (64.48%) as compared to those residing in the urban areas in whose case the corresponding percentage was 46.16%. The chi-square test also reveals a significant association between the two variables.

INCOME AND ECONOMIC REASONS

The economic reasons for low achievement were co-related with the income categories of parents/guardians of the low achievers and the analysis of data has been presented in Table 4.30.

Table 4.30: Distribution of low Achievers according to the Income Categories of their Parents/Guardians and the Economic Reasons

Income categories	Economic reasons		
	Low	**High**	**Total**
High and medium	22 (56.41%)	17 (43.59%)	39
Low	33 (37.08%)	56 (62.92%)	89
Total	**55**	**73**	**128**

$\chi^2 = 3.89$; df=1; p> 5.0

The analysis of data shown in the table indicates that a higher proportion of the low achievers whose family income was low considered economic factors as very important for their low academic performance (62.92%) as compared to those belonging to medium and high income categories in whose case the corresponding percentage was 43.59%. The chi-square test also shows a significant association between the two variables. This finding seems quite obvious because the students from the lower income group are likely to face a number of problems which directly affect their academic performance. For example, the students from the strata may not find it feasible to buy costly books or to take tuitions. The chi-square test also depicts a significant association between the two variables.

CASTE AND ECONOMIC REASONS

The economic reasons mentioned by the low achievers were further co-related with their caste background and the analysis of data has been presented in Table 4.31.

Table 4.31: Distribution of low achievers according to the caste background and the economic reasons

Caste Background	Economic Reason		
	Low	High	Total
High and medium	47 (48.96%)	49 (51.04%)	96
Low	8 (25.00%)	24 (75.00%)	32
Total	**55**	**73**	**128**

$\chi^2 = 5.61$; df= 1; p> 2.5

The analysis of data presented in the table reveals that three-fourths of the low achievers belonging to the low caste group considered economic reasons as very important for their low academic performance whereas about one half of the respondents belonging to medium and high caste groups expressed this view. The chi-square test also shows a significant association between the two variables.

❑ ❑ ❑ ❑ ❑

CHAPTER - V

SUMMARY AND CONCLUSION

As described in the introductory chapter, the main objective of the present study was to explore the impact of social inequalities on the levels of achievement motivation and academic performance of college students. In order to find out the differences in the above mentioned aspects for rural and urban areas, two colleges were selected, one each from these two areas. Besides the rural-urban dimension, the other variables of inequality taken into account are gender, educational levels of the family, occupation of parents/ guardians, family income, caste background and the type of family of the respondents. Thus, the above mentioned factors are the independent variables for the present study while academic performance and achievement motivation are the dependent variables. The null-hypotheses framed for the present research work state that the independent variables will not have a significant relationship with the dependent variables.

The objectives of the present study are as follows:

(i) To classify rural and urban college students with reference to various levels of achievement motivation and academic performance.

(ii) To find out the relationship of social factors (caste, educational level of family, type of family and place of residence), with achievement motivation and academic performance of the college students.

(iii) To explore the relationship of economic factors (occupational structure and income level of family) with achievement motivation and academic performance.

(iv) To find out the reasons for variations in the levels of academic performance of the students.

The following null hypotheses have been put to test in the present study.

1. There will be no significant difference in the need achievement and academic performance of rural and urban students.
2. There will be no gender differences in the need achievement and academic performance of college students.
3. There will be no difference with regard to the impact of socio-economic status on need achievement and academic performance.
4. There might not be significant differences in the levels of achievement motivation of arts and commerce students.
5. The educational levels of the respondents' families might not have a significant influence on academic performance and level of achievement motivation.

The thesis has been divided into four chapters besides the present one. The first chapter is introductory which includes statement of the research problem, conceptual and theoretical framework, the review of literature, objectives of the study, hypotheses and methodology of the study. The second chapter depicts the socio-economic profile of the respondents. The third chapter analyses the social factors affecting achievement motivation. The fourth chapter highlights the socio-economic correlates of academic performance.

The socio-economic profile has revealed the following characteristics of the respondents and their families:

(a) As the present study was confined to the college students, all the respondents were from the young age group. However, 39% of them had not reached the adulthood stage while the remaining 61% were adults (above 18 years of age).

(b) As the proportional random sample was drawn from among male and female students, there were an equal number of students from these two categories in the sample.

(c) An equal number of students, that is, 150 each was included in the sample from the rural and the urban colleges.

(d) An equal number of students were included in the sample from the three classes of B.A. and other three from B.Com course.

(e) Almost half of the respondents' families received medium educational scores and only 7.33% received low scores. The remaining 42.33% received high educational scores. The analysis revealed that a higher proportion of the urban families were placed in the high educational score category.

(f) A higher proportion of the parents/guardians of the respondents were engaged in low status jobs, closely followed by those who were engaged in business. Very few of them were engaged in high status jobs and agriculture.

(g) A higher proportion of parents/guardians of the respondents were placed in the middle income category, followed by those in the low income category. Only one fifth of the parents/guardians were in the high income category. A higher proportion of urban respondents were placed in the high income category as compared to the rural residents.

(h) A little more than half of the respondents belonged to medium status castes while the remaining were almost equally distributed in the high and low status caste categories. A higher proportion of the rural respondents belonged to the low caste groups.

(i) A majority of the respondents belonged to Hindu families (63%) while a little over one third of the respondents were from Sikh families. There were only five respondents from Muslim families.

A majority of the respondents were residing in the nuclear families (62.33%) while 37.67% belonged to joint and quasi joint families.

For the purpose of classifying the respondents in different categories of achievement motivation, they were administered a scale standardized by Asha Bhatnagar. Based on the scores received by the respondents on the basis of their responses to the statements of this scale, they were divided into three categories of achievement motivation. The analysis of data revealed that about two third of the respondents were placed in the medium category while the remaining were distributed in the high and low achievement categories. The achievement motivation categories were cross tabulated with the independent variables and the findings have been summarized below:

(a) There were no substantial differences in the achievement motivation levels of male and female students.

(b) No significant difference was found in the levels of achievement motivation among the students of 'Arts' and 'Commerce' streams.

(c) A higher proportion of the rural respondents received high motivation scores as compared to those residing in the urban areas.

(d) A higher proportion of the respondents whose parents/ guardians were engaged in low status jobs received high motivation scores as compared to those whose parents/ guardians were in high status jobs.

(e) A higher proportion of the respondents from the low income families received higher motivation scores as compared to those from the high and medium income families.

(f) A higher proportion of the respondents whose families had received medium and high educational scores were placed in the high achievement motivation category. There was only one respondent whose family had received low educational score, who was placed in the high motivation category.

(g) The analysis of data revealed that there were no substantial differences in the levels of achievement motivation of the respondents belonging to various caste categories.

(h) There were no significant differences in the levels of achievement motivation of the respondents belonging to different religious groups.

(i) There were no significant differences in the levels of achievement motivation of the respondents residing in different types of families.

The respondents were also asked a few questions having a bearing on achievement motivation. The findings with respect to these questions are as follows:

(a) A significant majority of the respondents liked their teachers.

(b) A higher proportion of the rural respondents liked their teachers as compared to the urban residents.

(c) A higher proportion of respondents whose parents/ guardians were engaged in lower status jobs mentioned that they liked their teachers.

The respondents were asked to respond to a question related to their perception about the importance of education. The findings with regard to this aspect are as follows:

(a) The analysis of data revealed that less than half of the respondents perceived the importance of education.

(b) A higher proportion of the urban respondents perceived the importance of education.

(c) A higher proportion of the 'Arts' students perceived the importance of education as compared to the 'Commerce' students.

The respondents were also asked to respond to a question indicating their liking about studies. The findings in this context are as follows:

(a) About two-thirds of the respondents did not like their studies as they mentioned that they would be pleased to miss their classes.

(b) A higher proportion of the female respondents were not in favour of missing their classes as compared the male respondents.

(c) A higher proportion of the rural respondents did not want to miss their classes as compared to the urban respondents.

(d) A higher proportion of the 'Arts' students were not in favour of missing their classes as compared to the 'commerce' students.

(e) A higher proportion of the respondents whose parents/guardians' income was less did not want to miss their classes as compared to those whose parents/guardians had medium or a high income.

In order to find out the desire for learning, the respondents were asked whether they enjoyed reading or not. The findings in this context are as follows:

(a) A majority of the respondents reported that they did not enjoy reading.

(b) A higher proportion of the female respondents enjoyed reading as compared to the male respondents.

(c) A higher proportion of the respondents from the rural areas enjoyed reading as compared to the urban respondents.

(d) A significantly higher proportion of the respondents whose families had received high educational scores enjoyed reading as compared to those whose families had received low and medium educational scores.

(e) A higher proportion of the respondents whose families had low income enjoyed reading as compared to those whose families were placed in the medium and high income categories.

Another aspect which has been probed in the present study relates to the academic performance of the respondents. The findings in this context have been summarized below:

(a) The highest proportion of the respondents were placed in the low academic performance category followed by those in the medium category. The lowest proportion of the respondents were placed in the high academic performance category.

(b) A higher proportion of the respondents who were upto 18 years of age were placed in the high academic performance category as compared to those who were in the age category of above 18 years.

(c) A significantly higher proportion of the female respondents were placed in the high and medium academic performance categories as compared to the male respondents.

(d) A higher proportion of the urban respondents received medium and high academic performance scores as compared to the rural respondents.

(e) A significantly higher proportion of 'Arts' students received high and medium academic performance scores as compared to the 'Commerce' students.

(f) A higher proportion of the respondents whose families had received high educational scores were placed in the high and medium academic performance categories.

(g) A slightly higher proportion of the respondents whose parents/guardians had low income were placed in medium and high categories of academic performance.

(h) The analysis of data revealed that there were no significant differences in the levels of academic performance of the respondents belonging to various caste categories.

The respondents were asked to respond to some statements related to seriousness about their studies. The analysis of data indicated that a higher proportion of the respondents were placed in the high category, closely followed by those in the medium category. Very few of the respondents had a low level of seriousness about studies. The seriousness about studies was correlated with other independent variables and the significant findings are as follows:

(a) A significantly higher proportion of the female respondents were placed in the high category as compared to the male respondents.

(b) A higher proportion of the rural respondents were placed in the high category as compared to the urban respondents.

(c) About two-third of the respondents whose families had received high educational scores were placed in the high category.

(d) A higher proportion of the respondents whose parents/ guardians belonged to the low income category were placed in the high category.

An attempt has also been made in the present study to find out the reasons for low academic performance of the students. First of all the respondents were asked to respond to certain statements depicting their attitude towards college. The analysis of data revealed that about 60% of them did not have a positive attitude towards their college. The attitude towards college was co-related with the independent variables and the significant findings are as follows:

(a) A higher proportion of the female low achievers had a positive attitude towards their college as compared to the male low achievers.

(b) A higher proportion of the low achievers from the rural areas had a favourable attitude towards their college as compared to those from the whom areas.

(c) A higher proportion of the low achievers whose parents/guardians were placed in the low income category had a favourable attitude towards their college as compared to those whose families had medium or high incomes.

The respondents were also asked to respond to some statements related to their housing conditions. The analysis of data revealed that about two-thirds of the low achievers were of the view that the housing problem was not an important reason for their low academic performance. The views of the low achievers about the housing problem were co-related with the independent variables and some of the significant findings are as follows:

(a) A higher proportion of the female low-achievers considered housing as a serious problem as compared to the male low achievers.

(b) A higher proportion of the low achievers from the rural areas perceived housing problem to be serious as compared to the urban low achievers.

(c) A considerably higher proportion of the low achievers whose parents/guardians had low incomes considered housing to be a serious problem as compared to those whose families were placed in the medium and high income categories.

The low achievers were also asked to respond to certain statements related to their health. The analysis of data revealed that about three-fourths of the low achievers did not consider health to be a major cause for their low academic performance. The views of the low achievers about their health problems were further co-related with the independent variables. Some of the significant findings in this respect are as follows:

(a) A significantly higher proportion of the urban low achievers considered health to be a major problem as compared to the rural low achievers.

(b) A higher proportion of the low achievers from low income families perceived health as a major problem as compared to those whose families had medium or high incomes.

The low achievers were asked to respond to certain statements in order to find out whether the psychological reasons were responsible for their low academic performance. The analysis of data revealed that a little more than half of the respondents considered psychological reasons to be significant for their low academic performance. The views of the low achievers in the context were co-related with the independent variables and the significant findings are as follows:

(a) A higher proportion of the male low achievers considered psychological reasons as more important than the female low achievers.

(b) A higher proportion of low achievers residing in the rural areas perceived psychological problems as more serious as compared to those residing in the urban areas.

(c) A higher proportion of those low achievers whose families had received low and medium educational scores perceived psychological problems to be more serious as compared to those from better educated families.

(d) A higher proportion of the low achievers from low income families reported more psychological problems as compared to those who belonged to medium and high income families.

The low achievers were also asked to respond to some statements related to their sphere of social interaction. The analysis of data revealed that almost the same proportion of the low achievers were placed in the two categories of limited and wider sphere of social interaction. The pattern of social interaction of the low achievers was cross-tabulated with the independent variables and the significant findings are as follows:

(a) A higher proportion of the low achievers residing in urban areas had wider sphere of social interaction as compared to the rural residents.

(b) A higher proportion of the respondents belonging to medium and high income families had a wider sphere of social interaction as compared to those belonging to low income families.

(c) A higher proportion of the low achievers belonging to medium and high caste groups had a wider sphere of social interaction as compared to those belonging to low caste groups.

The low achievers were further asked to respond to a few statements regarding their economic conditions. The analysis of data revealed that a little more than half of the low achievers considered economic reasons as quite important for their low academic performance. The views of the low achievers in this context were cross-tabulated with the independent variables and the significant findings are as follows:

(a) A higher proportion of the low achievers residing in the rural areas considered economic reasons as very important for their low academic performance as compared to the urban residents.

(b) A higher proportion of the low achievers from the low income families considered economic reasons as very significant as compared to those belonging to medium and high income families.

(c) About three-fourths of the low achievers belonging to the low caste group considered economic reasons as very important for their low academic performance, while only one fourth belonging to medium and high caste groups mentioned economic reasons as an important factor for their low academic performance.

The major findings of the present study have been reported in the preceding pages. Based on these findings a few conclusions can be drawn which have been presented in the ensuing paragraphs.

A number of null-hypotheses were formulated which have been put to test in the present research work. The first hypothesis stated that there will be no significant difference in the need achievement of rural and urban students. However, the findings of the present study do not substantiate this null-hypothesis. The findings indicate that the students from the rural areas had a higher n-Ach as compared to the urban students. Another finding of the present research work also reveals that a higher proportion of the rural students were more serious about their studies as compared to the urban students. This might be explained in terms of the fact that the students belonging to the rural areas have a strong desire to compete with the urban students.

The second null-hypothesis stated that there will be no gender differences with regard to achievement motivation. The findings of the study also do not reveal any substantial differences in the achievement motivation levels of male and female students. Thus, this finding is in conformity with the null-hypothesis in this context.

The third null-hypothesis stated that there will be no differences with regard to the impact of socio-economic status on need-achievement. However, the findings of the present research work revealed that the students belonging to the families with lower incomes received higher motivational scores as compared to those belonging to medium and high income families. This finding indicates a desire among the students belonging to lower economic strata to compete with the students of the upper strata. However, no substantial differences were found in the levels of achievement motivation of the respondents belonging to various caste categories. Thus, it can be concluded that caste inequality does not influence the levels of n-Ach to a great extent whereas the economic inequalities are more significant in this context.

The fourth null-hypothesis stated that there might not be significant differences in the levels of achievement motivation of 'Arts' and 'Commerce' students. The findings of the present study are in conformity with this null-hypothesis. However, the analysis indicates that the proportion of 'Arts' students was a little higher in the high achievement motivation category as compared to the 'Commerce' students, but this difference is not statistically significant to conclude that there are differences among students of these two streams of study with regard to their n-Ach.

The fifth null-hypothesis stated that the educational levels of the respondents' families might not have a significant influence on the levels of their achievement motivation. However, the findings of the present book have not corroborated this null-hypothesis. The findings clearly indicate that a higher proportion of the students belonging to better educated families depict a trend towards achievement of excellence as compared to the students from less educated families.

The null-hypotheses described above are also related with the academic performance of the respondents. The findings of the present study indicate that the urban students had a better academic performance as compared to the rural students. Thus the findings do not corroborate the null-hypothesis in this context.

The null-hypothesis with regard to gender and levels of academic performance has also not been substantiated by the analysis of data. The findings clearly indicate that the female respondents had a higher level of academic performance as compared to the male respondents.

The null-hypothesis with regard to the impact of socio-economic status on the academic performance of the respondents has been partially substantiated by the findings. The income categories of respondents' families were not significantly co-related with their academic performance. However, a slightly higher proportion of the respondents belonging to low income families have received high academic performance scores. Similarly, the analysis of data did not reveal any significant differences in the levels of academic performance of the respondents belonging to various caste categories.

The findings with regard to the relationship between field of study and levels of academic performance clearly indicate that the 'Arts' students had higher levels of academic performance as compared to the 'Commerce' students. Thus the null-hypothesis in this context has not been confirmed by the present research work.

The null-hypothesis regarding the relationship between the academic performance of the respondents and the levels of education of their families has not been substantiated by the findings of the study. The findings amply demonstrate that the students from better educated families were placed in the higher levels of academic performance as compared to those belonging to less educated families.

Some other dimensions related to the academic performance of the students were also investigated in order to find out the reasons for low academic achievement. The findings revealed that a majority of the male and urban students and those belonging to economically well-off families did not have a positive attitude towards their college. Most of the students considered housing to be a major reason for their low academic performance. The female and rural respondents and those belonging to economically poor families were more concerned about the housing problem. Health was not considered as a very serious problem by most of the low academic performers. The psychological reasons for low academic performance were considered more important by the male and rural respondents and those from the lower economic strata. The social interaction pattern of the low achievers revealed that the rural, the economically poor and those respondents who belonged to lower caste groups had a limited sphere of social interaction. The economic reasons for low academic performance were generally mentioned by the respondents from rural areas, from poor families and those from low caste families.

BIBLIOGRAPHY

Abbasayulu, Y.B. (1978) *Impact of Higher Education among the Scheduled Caste, Scheduled Tribe and Backward Class Students in Osmania University Jurisdiction*, Research Project sponsored by Osmania University, mimeographed.

Agarwal, S.C. and Singh, S. (2004) "Achievement motivation of co-educational and single sex educational secondary students." *Indian Journal of Psycholmetry and Education*, 35(1), 26-31.

Aggarwal, Y.P. and Saini, V.P. (1969) "Pattern of Study Habits and Its Relationship with Achievements and Parents Economic and Educational Status. *J. Edul. Res. and Extn.*, 5(4), 159 64.

Aggarwal, V.P. and Suraksha (1981) "Achievement Motivation at High Level of Perception of Personal Control", *Indian Psychological Abstracts,* 18(1).

Aikara, J. (1979) *Educating out-of-school Children: A Survey of Dharavi Slum,* Bombay: Tata Institute of Social Sciences, Unpublished Thesis.

Aikara, J. (1980) *Scheduled Castes and Higher Education: A Study of College Students in Bombay*, Poona: Dastane Ramachandra.

Alderman, R.B. (1974) *Psychological Behaviour in Sports.* Philadelphia: Saunders.

Allwords Dictionary (2006) "Definitions of Intelligence." *http:/ /www.idsia.ch.*

Atkinson, J. W. (1953) "The Achievement Motive and Recall of Interrupted and Completed Tasks: *Journal of Experimental Psychology*, 46, 381-390.

Atkinson, J.W. (1958) (ed.) *Motives in Fantasy, Action and Society*, New York: Van Nostrand.

Atkinson, J.W. (1964) *An Introduction to Motivation*. Princeton: Nostrand.

Atkinson, J.W. (1968) Achievement motivation, In: D.L. Sills (ed.) International *Encyclopaedia of the Social Sciences.* New York: Macmillan and Free Press, pp. 27-33.

Atkinson, J.W. (1957) "Motivational Determinants of Risk-taking Behaviour." *Psychological Review*, 64, 359-372.

Atkinson, J.W. and Feather, N.T. (1966) *A Theory of Achievement Motivation,* New York, John Willey and Sons. Inc.

Atkinson, J.W. and Litwin, G.H. (1960) "Achievement Motivation and Test Anxiety Conceived as Motive to Approach Success and Motive to Avoid Failure." *Journal Abnormal and Social Psychology,* pp. 52-53.

Barial, R.N.P. (1966) "An Investigation into the Impact of Social Class Background Upon Achievement and Motivation" Ph.D. Thesis, Punjabi University, Patiala.

Begum T.S. and Phukan, M (2005) "Correlation Between Academic Achievement and Intelligence." *Indian Psychological Review*, 65, 257-259.

Bentham, J. (1879) *Principles of Morals and Legislation*, Oxford Caredon Press.

Buck, R. (1958) *Motives in Fantasy, Action and Society*, New York: Van Nostrand.

Carter, H.D. (1940) "The Development of Vocational Attitude", *J. Cons. Psychology*, Vol. 4, 185-191.

Cattell, R.B. (1965) *The Scientific Analysis of Personality*. Baltimore: Penguin.

Chauhan, S.S. (1982) "A Study of Academic Motivation in Relation to Intelligence and Socio-economic Status." *Journal of Educational Research and Extension,* 19(1).

Chitnis, Suma (1974) "Sociology of Education: A Trend Report", In: *Survey of Research in Sociology and Social Anthropology*, Vol. II.

Chitnis, Suma (1977) "Education and Equality", In: A Kiloskowska and G. Martinotti (eds.) *Education in a Changing Society*, London; Sage Publications, pp. 73-106.

Chitnis, Suma (1981) "A Long Way to Go": *Report on a Survey of Scheduled Caste High School and College Students in Fifteen States of India*, New Delhi: Allied.

Chitnis, Suma and Altbach, P.G. (eds.), (1979) *The Indian Academic A Profession: Crisis and Change in the Teaching Community*, Delhi: Macmillan.

Choudhary, Nirmala (1971) *The Relationship Between Achievement motivation and Anxiety, Intelligence, Sex, Social Class and Vocaboral Aspirations*. Ph.D. Thesis, Department of Psychology, Panjab University, Chandigarh.

Clarence, M. (1978) "The Effect of Achievement Motivation and Socio-economic Background on the Earnings of Youngmen" *Dissertation Abstracts International*. 39, 1712 A.

Colman and Andrew, M. (2005) "Dictionary of Psychology." *Oxford University Press.*

Cox, C.C. (1962) "The Early Mental Traits of Three Hundred Geniuses" In: L.M. Torman (Ed.) *Genetic Studies of Genius*. Stanford University Press, Vol. II.

Crandall, V.J. (1963) Achievement, *in H. Stevenson (Ed.) Child Psychology, Sixty Second Year Book of the National Society for Study of Education*, Chicago, University of Chicago Press.

D'Souza, V.S. (1977) 'Spatial Patterns of Educational Disparities in Towns: A Case Study a District of Punjab'. *Social Action*, 27(4), 369-78.

De, B and Priya, S. (1972) "Some Personal and Academic Correlates of Achievement Motivation", *Indian Journal of Psychology*, 47, 55-64.

Desai, A.R. (1974) "Dilemma of Educational Development after Independence", *The New Era*, 55(8), 213- 25.

Dewan, Sonia (1996) A Comparative Study of Academic Achievement, Family Environment, Classroom Environment, Achievement Motivation and Intelligence of Senior Secondary Students of Different Socio-economic Groups, Ph.D. Thesis, Panjab University, Chandigarh.

Donals, J.S. (1983) "Achievement Motivation as a Factor Related to the Diagnostic Problem Solving Effectiveness of Students of Auto Motive Technology." *Dissertation Abstracts International*, 43(7).

Drever, James (1952) *A Dictionary of Psychology*, Penguin Books.

Dutt, N.K. and Sabharwal V.K., (1973) "A Study of Achievement Motivation to School Subjects, Socio-economic Status of Parents and Sex." *Journal of Education Psychology*, Vol. 31.

Freud, S. (1920) *A General Introduction to Psychoanalysis*. New York; Liverright.

Fox B., Robert (1969) "The Relationship of Achievement Motivation to Sex, Achievement, Intelligence, Socio-economic Status and Level of Educational Aspiration for Eighth Grade Group". *Dissertation Abstracts International*, 30, 1331A.

Gakhar, S.C. (2004) "Acquisition of Geographical Concepts in Relation to Intelligence, Socio-economic Status and Personality Variables." *Psycho-Lingua,* 34 (1), 47-49.

Gokulnathan, P.P. (1972) A Study of Achievement Related Motivation (n-Achievement and Anxiety) and Educational Achievement Among Secondary School Pupils. Ph.D. Thesis, Dibrugarh University.

Gokulnathan, P.P. and Prayag Mehta (1972) "Achievement Motive in Tribal and Non-tribal Assamese Secondary School Adolescent." *Educational Review*, 7(1), 67-68.

Good-Carter, V. (1959) *Dictionary of Education.* Second Edition, McGraw-Hill, New York, pp. 493-510.

Gore, M.S., (1977c) *Indian Youth: Processes of Socialization*, New Delhi, Viswa Yuvak Kendra.

Goswami R. (1969) "School Teacher as a Determinant of Educability in India: A Sociological Study", In: S.P. Ruhela (ed.) *Social Determinants of Educability in India,* Jain, New Delhi, pp. 95-106.

Gupta, J.P. and Gupta, V.K. (1970) *A Study of Anxiety and Achievement Motivation in Relation to Sex and Socio-economic Status.* Research Monographs, Sohan Lal College of Education, Ambala City.

Gupta, P.L. (1989) "Study of 9th Class Boys and Girls in Relation to Their Achievement Motivation and Academic Achievement." *The Educational Review*, 95(1), 1-4.

Hebb, D.O. (1972) *Textbook of Psychology*. Philadelphia: W.B. Saunders.

Heckhausen, H. (1967) *The Anatomy of Achievement Motivation*. New York: Academic Press.

ICSSR, (1974) Survey of Research in Sociology and Social Anthropology, Vol. II, Satvahan Publications, New Delhi.

Ismail, Y. (1982) "A Study of Relationship Between Achievement Motivation and Learning Styles of a Group of Malaysia Students Attending Northern Illinois University." *Dissertation Abstracts International*, 43(7), p. 204.

Jerrath, J.M. (1970) A Study of Personality Correlates of Need Achievement. Unpublished. M.A. Thesis, Panjab University, Chandigarh.

Jesudasan, Victor (1972) "Some Descriptive Characteristics of Indian Students in The United States 1954-55 to 1966-70", Indian Journal of Sociology. 3 (1-2), 119-38. 2333.

Jyothi, P. (1984) "A Study of Achievement Motivation in Relation to Personality Dimension and Performance Among High and Low Achieving College Girls". *Journal of Psychological Research*, 28(3), 135.

Kamala, S. (1983) "Achievement Motivation in Relation to Masculinity-Feminity". *Psychological Studies*, 28(1), 81.

Katz, I. (1967) "The Socialization of Academic Motivation in Minority Group Children", In: D. Levine (ed.) *Nebraska Symposium on Motivation,* Lincoln, Nebraska, University of Nebraska Press.

Kaur, A., Gakhar, S.C. and Kaur, N. (2004) "A Study of Select Intellectual and Non-intellectual Correlates of Scientific Attitude," *Sikhiya Khoj Pattar* 3, 46-48.

Kaur, Jagbir (1972) "Need Achievement, Study Habits and Socio-economic Status of 10th Class Students of Patiala District", M.A. Thesis, Punjabi University, Patiala.

Kaur, J. (2004) "Achievement Motivation of Student,". *Sikhiya Khoj Pattar* 3. 19-21.

Kaur, Parminder (1993) A Study of Vocational Interests of 10+1 Class Students in Relation to Their Intelligence and Academic Achievement. M. Phil. (Psychology), Punjabi University. Patiala.

Kaur, Satpal (1973) A Study of Need Achievement in Relation to Personality Adjustment of College Students, Unpublished M.A. Thesis, Punjabi University, Patiala.

King, A.D. (1970) "Elite Education and the Economy": IIT Entrance, *Economic and Political Weekly*, 5(35), 1463-71.

Kiran, S.B. and Singh, Amrik (1984) "Effect of Parental Education, Economic Status and Academic Stream on the Achievement Motivation". *Journal of the Institute of Educational Research*, 8, 21.

Klinger, E. (1971) *Structure and Functions of Fantasy.* New York: Willey Inter Sciences.

Koteswara M.N. and Reddy Ramachandra B. (2001) A Comparative Study of the Characteristics of High Achievers and Low Achievers in Reading of Class VIII Pupils with Special with Special Reference to School and Home Factors. M. Phil. Dissertation in Education, Sri Venkateswara University.

Krishanamurthy (2001) "Achievement as Related to Academic Achievement Motivation and Attitude Towards Study of History," 27, 34-36. *Educational Review,* 106(5-6), 95, 99.

Lesser, G.S., Krawitz Thoda N. and Packard Rota (1963) "Experimental Arousal of Achievement Motivation in Adolescent Girls" *Journal of Abnormal and Social Psychology*, 66, 59-66.

Lowell, E.L. (1950) A Methodological Study of Projectively Measured Achievement Motivation. Unpublished Master's thesis, Wesleym University.

Maltesha, R.N. (1969) "A Study of the Relationship Between n- Achievement-n-Affiliation, n-power and Socio-economic Status, *Indian Journal of Experimental Psychology* 3(2), 31-33.

McClelland, D.C. (1951) *Personality*. New York: Dryden Press.

McClelland, D.C. (1961) *The Achieving Society*. Princeton, N.J.: Van Nostrand.

McClelland, *et al.* (1953) *The Achievement Motive*. New York; Appletion-century-Crofts.

McClelland, D.C. (1955) "Some Social Consequences of Achievement Motivation" In: M.R. Jones (ed.) *Nebraska Symposium on Motivation*, Lincoln, Nebraska: University of Nebraska Press.

McGill, D.W. (1979) "Test Performance as a Function of Socio-economic Status. Achievement Motivation and Type of Reward". *Dissertation Abstract International*, 39, 4892 A.

Mehta, P. (1969) *The Achievement Motive in High School Boys,* New Delhi, NCERT.

Morrison, William A. (1959) "Family Types in Badalpur : An Analysis of a Changing Institution in Maharashtrian Village", *Sociological Bulletin*, 8(2), 45-67.

Mubayi, G. (1976) A Study of Achievement Motive of Secondary School Pupils of Scheduled Tribes of South Gujarat, Ph.D. Thesis, M.S. University, Baroda.

Murry, H.A. (1938), *Explorations in Personality*, New York: Oxford University Press.

Naik (2002) "Place of Motivation in Learning". *Journal of the Education Review*, p. 939.

Newcomle, T.H. (1950) *Social Psychology*, The Drydren Press, New York.

Patel, A.D. (1977) The Study of Achievement Motive, Anxiety, Performance at the University Examination and Socio-economic Status of Student-teacher in the Colleges of Education in the State of Gujarat, Ph.D. Thesis, Sardar Patel University, Gujarat.

Pathak, A.B. and Shukla, R.P. (1985) "A Study of Aspiration and Achievement Motivation of Scheduled Caste Student-teachers". *Journal of Education and Psychology*, 42(4), 196.

Pathania R., Kaur P. and Pathania P. (2005) "Problems Faced by the Tribal Students in Education." *The Indian Journal of Social Work,* 66(3), 323-333.

Patil, M.V., Gaonkar, V. and Kataki, P.A. (1994) "Sex Role Perception of Adolescents as Influenced by Self-concept and Achievement Motivation." *Psychological Studies,* 39(1), 37-39.

Rao, S.N. (1965) "Student's Performance in Relation to some Aspects of Personality and Academic Adjustment" in Survey of Research in Education, M.S. University, Baroda.

Reddy, V.E. and Bhatt, K.S. (1977) *The Out of School Youth,* New Dehli : Sterling.

Ruhela, S.P. (1972-75) *Education and the Indian Working Class,* Project Sponsored by U.G.C., New Delhi: Teachers College, Jamia Millia Islamia, New Delhi.

Sandhu, Paramjit Kaur (1985) A Study of Need Achievement of Rural and Urban 10th Grade Students in Relation to Certain Socio-economic Variables and Sex. M.Phil. (Edu.), Punjabi University. Patiala.

Sears, R.R. (1942) "Success and failure: A Study of Mobility", In: S. NcNewar and M. Merill (eds.) *Studies in Personality,* New York: McGraw Hill.

Shan, H.R. (2003) "Academic Achievement Among High School Students of Jammu in Relation to Intelligence and Creative Thinking, Insight." *Journal of Applied Research in Education,* 9(1), 10-16.

Sharma, B., Subramaniam and Narayana (2006), "Relationships Between Self-concept, Achievement Motivation and Achievement in Mathematics: A Gender Comparison." *Edutracks* 5(9), 29-32.

Sharma and Singhal (1969) "Parental Occupation and School Achievement", *Quest in Education*, 6(4), 1-4.

Sharma, Mamta (1992) Changes in Psycho Physiological Response of Normal Individual under the Influence of Preferred Music and Academic Discipline. M. Phil. (Psychology), Punjabi University, Patiala.

Sharma, Dev Dutt (1968) Bhil Students Between Tradition and Change: A Study in the Role of Education, University of Udaipur, Udaipur.

Shrivastava P.K. and Tiwari M.L. (1967) "Socio-Economic Stratification and need-achievements, *Psychological Studies*, 12, 7-16.

Singh A.J. and Kumar, Bachan (1977) "Relationship of Need-Achievement with Personality Groups". *Indian Educational Review*. 12(4), 79-86.

Singh, V. and Kaur, A. (2003) "Achievement Motivation Pare Background as the Determinations of Students Academic Achievement." *The Educational Review*. 46(09), 174-176.

Suchdeva, M.S. (2006) Essentials of Educational Technology and Management. Patiala: Twenty First Century Publications.

Teevan, R.C. and McGhee, P.E. (1972) "Childhood Development of Fear of Failure Motivation." *Journal of Personality and Social Psychology*, 2, 345-348.

Trow, W.C. (1960) *Psychology in Teaching and Learning*. Boston: Houghton Mifflin Co. The Riverside Press, Cambridge.

Vidhu, Mohan (1972) Academic Achievement: A Review of Its Determinants. *Journal of Education and Psychology*, 29(4), 251-257.

Wilson, (1993) The Effect of Motivational Orientation and Self-concept of Ability on Academic Achievement of African American Students, Ph.D. Thesis, University of Georgia, 132 pp. DAI, 53(9), 3150A.

Winterbottom, M.R., (1958) The Relation of Need for Achievement to Learning Experience in Independence and Mastery, in J.W. Atkinson (ed.) *Motives in Fantasy, Action and Society*. Princeton, N.J.O. Nostrand Co., pp. 53-70.

Yadav, P.K. (1979) *A study of Motives for Vocation Preferences of Adolescents*. Ph.D. Thesis, Agra University, Agra.

Young, P.T. (1961) *Motivation and Emotion: A Survey of the Determinants of Human and Animal Activity*, New York: Wiley.

❑ ❑ ❑ ❑ ❑

Index

N

O

P

Q

R

S

T

V

❑❑❑